WHEN I WAS A KID, THIS WAS A FREE COUNTRY

WHEN I WAS A KID, THIS WAS A FREE COUNTRY

G. GORDON LIDDY

Since 1947
REGNERY PUBLISHING, INC.
An Eagle Publishing Company • Washington, DC

Copyright © 2002 by G. Gordon Liddy

Lyric excerpt from "Courtesy of the Red, White, and Blue (The Angry American)," words by Toby Keith, © 2002 Tokeco Tunes

Library of Congress Cataloging-in-Publication Data

Liddy, G. Gordon.
  When I was a kid, this was a free country / G. Gordon Liddy.
     p. cm.
Includes index.
  ISBN 0-89526-175-8 (acid-free paper)
  1. United States—Civilization—Philosophy. 2. United States—
Civilization—1945– 3. National characteristics, American. 4. United
States—Politics and government—1989– 5. Civil rights—United States.
6. Liddy, G. Gordon. I. Title.
  E169.1 .L5394 2002
  973'.01—dc21

                                        2002007450

Published in the United States by
Regnery Publishing, Inc.
An Eagle Publishing Company
One Massachusetts Avenue, NW
Washington, DC 20001

Visit us at www.regnery.com

Distributed to the trade by
National Book Network
4720-A Boston Way
Lanham, MD 20706

Printed on acid-free paper
Manufactured in the United States of America

10 9 8 7 6 5 4 3 2 1

Books are available in quantity for promotional or premium use. Write to Director of Special Sales, Regnery Publishing, Inc., One Massachusetts Avenue, NW, Washington, DC 20001, for information on discounts and terms or call (202) 216-0600.

This book is dedicated to my mother,
MARIA ABBATICCHIO LIDDY,
who, at ninety-four and blind, cannot read it,
but will love it as she has always loved me—
anyway.

CONTENTS

FRANK SMITH RETURNS TO FRANCE

HIS NAME IS QUINTESSENTIALLY AMERICAN, Frank Smith.

He and his wife, Betty, were among those assigned, with me, to table 47 for the second seating at dinner aboard the cruise ship *Maasdam,* which was temporarily docked at Le Havre while cruising European waters. Although from his looks I guessed Frank was retired, I asked what he did for a living. He answered politely, saying that these days he just worked half a day, and returned to his meal, seemingly preoccupied.

Betty was seated next to me and filled me in: Frank is a tool-and-die maker, a master machinist, the elite of the blue-collar world. He has his own two-man machine shop (down from twenty-two men because he got fed up with government regulations), and he takes only the most difficult jobs. His idea of "half a day" is twelve hours. This cruise was a gift to Frank and Betty from their daughter and son-in-law, Ann and Joe Murphy, who accompanied them. Joe is a retired pharmacist.

I mentioned that I was going to take a tour of the Normandy beaches where the Americans landed on 6 June 1944. I had been, I explained, "going on fourteen" that day. When the older boys in town had come back, they had told me they were there but that was all. "Frank's going back, too," Ann said. Thinking that perhaps Frank had taken the tour before, I asked him, "When were you there last?"

Frank didn't look up from his plate. "Fifty-three years ago," he said.

"Dad's been real quiet since he decided to go back," Ann said. He's entitled to be, I thought, and I dropped the subject.

Early the next morning I asked Frank if I could sit next to him on the bus. He nodded his agreement and I took the aisle seat. As the bus pulled out, the tour guide began what was to be a daylong lecture, exceptionally well done, especially when one considers that the events he was describing happened ten years before he was born. The weather was beautiful as he pointed out the flat, hedge-rowed, pastoral lands that extended back from cliffs that overlooked the beaches and the sea. Our bus threaded its way through narrow village streets lined with buildings of thick and ancient stone. This was the land from which William, Duke of Normandy, in 1066 launched a successful invasion going the other way—to England—and became known as William the Conqueror.

This was *not* the way things looked on D-Day. The weather that day was foul; the wind was up; and to the fog of weather was added the fog of battle—the smoke of gunfire and the massive, earsplitting eruptions of high-explosive bombs and artillery shells. The lowlands behind the beaches had been flooded to a depth of three feet—enough to drown a heavily laden landing paratrooper. "Rommel's asparagus"—three-meter-high stakes wired together at the tops and rigged with explosives—lay in wait like a deadly spiderweb for any glider trying to land troops. Vast minefields awaited any survivors. The streets of the villages were century-old tank traps, setting the tankers up for the German soldiers' deadly *panzerfausten;* these one-man rockets could easily destroy the American Sherman tanks, which were so vulnerable anyway that the British called them "Ronsons" in reference to that cigarette lighter's ad of the day, "Lights first time, every time." The Germans called them "Tommy cookers" for the same reason.

On the cliffs, on the beaches, and out into the sea, the "Atlantic Wall" of Adolf Hitler's Fortress Europe extended: immense reinforced concrete gun emplacements, more three-meter stakes, and steel-and-concrete tetrahedrons. The German guns, from artillery to machine guns, had already been registered—azimuth and ranges to their targets—and preset exactly to slaughter anything or anyone trying to come ashore through the storm-roiled surf.

Our first stop was Pointe du Hoc, where 226 American Rangers were to use rocket-propelled grappling lines to scale the nearly sheer cliff and silence the German artillery in the massive concrete bunkers at the summit. The land is as the battle left it, save for the healing grass that covers the huge craters, and forms a setting for the crazily heaved concrete rubble. In the fog and smoke the Rangers went to the wrong point and had to fight their way back through the heaving waves under constant heavy enemy fire to the correct one, only to find that their rocket-propelled lines, now soaked with water, were useless. Under the merciless barrage, the Rangers clawed their way up the cliff face with their hands and feet, and, incredibly, took the emplacements.

The guns weren't there. Wooden dummies were in their place. The men who remained fought their way inland to a forest where the guns were hidden and put phosphorus grenades down their barrels to destroy them, thus accomplishing their objective. The Rangers took 66 percent casualties.

At Omaha Beach I found a German 88mm artillery piece still trained along the length of the beach, looking down the throats of the Americans who made it alive out of the pounding surf. It was the best artillery piece of any army in the war—a killer of anything from aircraft, as a *flugzeugabwehrkanone* (from which we get the term "flak"), to tanks. It's rusted now, with a monument built around and over it to the American National Guard units that landed there when it was clean, glistening with fresh oil, and sending lethal shells at them rapid-fire—at a velocity of three thousand feet per second.

The carnage began at sea when the troops had to descend rope cargo nets, then drop into the small boats waiting to deliver them to shore. Those who missed fell into the sea and, burdened with their packs, drowned. Others were delivered to sandbars way offshore. They drowned. Specially prepared tanks with "skirts" added to enable them to float were put into the heaving sea. Half promptly sank, drowning their crews. Paratroopers were dropped into the sea. They drowned. All cried out for help to the passing landing craft. None stopped to aid them. Orders.

Those who made it alive to the shore quickly lost their officers, then many noncoms. They ended up at the wrong place because of drifting boats, thus losing their objectives. Hellish fire tore into them from the cliffs above the beach. The wounded had to be given morphine shots while still in the water, then—lest they, too, drown—be dragged *into* the fire, *toward* the enemy. Officers and noncoms dead or dying, their objectives lost, the air thick with steel, fog, and smoke, the Americans knew what they had to do—storm the cliffs and kill the enemy before he killed all of them. Incredibly, they did just that. The cost of that *one day's* fighting was *200,000 dead* on all sides.

The American cemetery behind Omaha Beach is a beautifully kept place of rest for heroes. I left Frank alone as he pondered it. Wanting to photograph that holy place—holier than any of the great cathedrals I was to visit later—I walked between the rows of graves with their neat white crosses and Stars of David, praying for the dead and asking their pardon for walking on their resting places, and for having been just a few years too young to have been with them that terrible day.

Later, Frank and I went over to a small building where visitors could sign a guest book and, through the aid of a computer, locate the graves of friends, relatives, and comrades buried there. Frank was able to locate one fallen comrade with some difficulty. The young lady who was manning the computer was French and her English not all it might be. We had heard that there was a special guest book any American armed forces veteran could sign. It was nowhere in evidence, and requests by several men received no response from the computer operator.

I asked her for it in French and she promptly produced it. Frank and I signed it, I making sure by noting my dates of service during the Korean War that I would never be mistaken for one of the heroes of the greatest war in history, fought by the finest generation we have ever produced.

The lecturer had told us that as terrible as the battle was for those who stormed Omaha Beach, there was one outfit that went through even worse—the airborne. General Eisenhower had been prepared to accept *75 percent* casualties among the airborne troops who were called upon to drop behind the enemy lines on D-Day. His estimate was about right. I watched as Frank signed the veterans' book. His outfit was the Eighty-second Airborne Division and he had jumped with them on 6 June 1944.

To those who fight a war, all battles are small-unit actions. The smallest unit in the infantry is the eight-man squad. All day, as the tour guide had lectured, we had all looked out the bus windows to the left, toward the beach and the sea. Not Frank. He kept looking toward the right, seemingly trying to spot where his squad had landed, other times looking down, not seeing the beauty of the Normandy of today that was bought by those brave men more than half a century ago; his mind was seeing them buy it, minute by minute, wound by wound, life by life.

His daughter told me. Of all the men in the squad he jumped with on 6 June 1944, Frank Smith was the only one who made it out alive.

Frank Smith was one of more than 16 million men who served in the armed forces during World War II. Like Frank, the vast majority came of age during the Great Depression. Also like Frank, many of those who made it back from Europe and Asia went on to lead honorable lives, raising families and excelling in their chosen professions.

I lived through World War II, and I appreciate the sacrifices of our fine American soldiers now more than ever. As a boy I listened to President Roosevelt tell us that it would take the efforts of every man, woman, and child to win the war. He was right, and we knew it, which is so why many millions of men enlisted to fight, and why all of us at home pitched in. The nation was united as never before or since. The reason is simple. We knew that we were defending something important, that our nation stood for something great. Millions of soldiers, sailors, and airmen willingly went off to Europe and the Pacific to fight for the freedoms we are guaranteed under our Constitution—and indeed, many of them gave their lives for this country. This was the America in which I grew up.

You see, when I was a kid, this was a free country....

1

LIBERTIES LOST

WHEN I WAS A KID, THIS WAS A FREE COUNTRY. I remember it.

I have been watching, in sadness and anger, for over seventy years as our precious liberty has slipped ever faster from our grasp—and most people don't even know it's happening. Countless Americans—brave souls like Frank Smith—have sacrificed everything to defend our freedoms. But today it's as if Americans don't know what it is they are rapidly losing.

I, for one, *can* see it happening. In all the years I've done my radio program, I've heard countless horrifying tales of liberties lost. Five days a week, four hours a day, I converse with people of all ages, from all walks of life, from all over this vast nation— from Washington, D.C., in the east to Honolulu in the west, and from New Orleans in the south to Fairbanks in the north.

I am a member of the last generation to remember what this country was like when it was free. Once there is no longer such a generation, America will need new Jeffersons and Madisons to re-create this great nation in her original image. When I was a kid, my young buddies and I could walk down the street carrying a rifle, a handgun, or a shotgun that our dad or uncle had bought for us at the local hardware store, or through the mail (the way Bat Masterson bought his Colt revolvers). In the fall, the air would be redolent with the delicious aroma of leaves burning in the gutter. We'd head for the woods to hunt crow or just bang away at tin cans on a stick against a backstopping hill, or venture out to a farmer's fields for game birds. The farmer might be filling in a swamp on his land to make it productive. A man with a home on a riverbank might be cutting down a tree on his property because it blocked his view. When a car went past us, we competed against one another to see who could identify it first. Sometimes it was a challenge, because the car would be a European make, something the owner had shipped over because he liked how low and racy it was.

People were free to speak their minds, even if what they had to say was contemptible; people who didn't like it were free to say so in no uncertain terms—anywhere, particularly in that bastion of ideas, the university. Property owners felt secure in the knowledge that their possessions could not be taken from them, and at the very least that they would be afforded due process of law. Everyone knew that if he injured someone, he would be liable for the money it took to make that person whole, but confident that if he had not caused the injury he could not be held liable under the law. As to what was or was not criminal conduct, or for the settlement of civil disputes, citizens looked to the laws of their respective sovereign states.

On the Fourth of July we celebrated our liberty with parades and fireworks, and the kids participated as much as the grown-ups. My first march came in the 1930s as a member of the Sts. Peter and Paul Catholic grammar school Drum and Bugle Corps in Hoboken, New Jersey. After the parades, we kids would go out to a field and fire off the fireworks we'd purchased—display rockets, roman candles, and powerful firecrackers. For some of us, even that wasn't good enough. At a drugstore we'd buy sulfur and saltpeter (the kind Mom used for canning her garden produce), and from a hardwood fire we'd make our own charcoal and then crush it into a fine dust. Using a simple three-two-one formula, we'd make our own black powder and use an empty toilet paper roll to make a *real* firecracker.* Often we would buy two bolts and a nut from the hardware store. We'd cut the white tips off kitchen matches with a single-edged razor blade, turn one bolt into the nut just enough to hold, fill the gap with the match tips, then carefully (so it wouldn't go off while we were holding it) screw the other bolt in on top of the match tips. Throw that sucker end over end so she'd hit the street on either end, and— *wham!* My favorite was to buy metallic sodium, a metal that reacted to air and, violently, to water. You could get it either at the drugstore (it came in a glass jar filled with oil to keep it from reacting) or by mail from the company that made the chemistry sets we all got for Christmas. I'd wrap a chunk of it in a wad of cotton bound by string and throw it into deep water. It took a few moments, during which time the heavy sodium was sinking, for the water to saturate the cotton and get to the metal. *Boom!...*

---

* When, during my service in the Nixon administration, it fell to me to write the federal Explosives Control Act, I carved out a personal exemption for each citizen to possess five pounds of black powder.

These freedoms and more are gone now.

Today, commercially manufactured fireworks are forbidden to anyone other than professionals, and our homemade efforts would get us arrested under federal law for making "destructive devices."

In the name of fighting crime, mail-order sales of firearms are forbidden. This is a matter of indifference to criminals, of course; they simply steal firearms or buy them from other criminals. Nor can the local hardware store sell you the firearm you need to protect your family from such criminals; the proprietors would have to endure far too much federal bureaucratic nonsense and paperwork.

Burning leaves in the gutter or elsewhere is forbidden, the victim of bogus theories about "global warming"—something that, along with global cooling, occurs naturally in great cycles that last eons and have nothing to do with the piddling activities of humans.

Federal laws protect crows from harm, but not the farmer's seed corn from crows. Sorry about that, but birds are now more important than humans. Indeed, the farmer would be imprisoned for filling in the swamp he owns, because, you see, it is a "wetland"* and therefore a "navigable waterway" and thus under federal jurisdiction. Never mind that the only boat that

---

* "Wetland" is now the euphemism employed when what is meant is a swamp, just as "rain forest" is used instead of "jungle." It is just a way for environmentalist con men to get suckers to empty their pockets for their causes and vote for their candidates. These hustlers are smart enough to know that people would never rally to save a "swamp" or a "jungle." But "wetlands" and "rain forests"? That's an entirely different story.

could navigate it is better suited to a bathtub and a three-year-old captain. The riverbank and the tree may be on a man's property, but if the river is a tributary to a protected bay many miles away, the tree belongs to the government, which will assess him a huge fine if he cuts it down.

And forget about importing that European car you fancy. If it doesn't have an air bag that could kill your aged mother, your child, or your less-than-tall wife, it is forbidden entry.

Dare to laugh, while matriculating at an American university, at someone's idea or outlandish costume—much less challenge the thought that, say, women are equal to men in every respect and for every activity, regardless of size, strength, or plumbing—and risk expulsion.

God forbid the federal government should, however mistakenly, believe you have used your property to further an allegedly illegal purpose—or even that someone else has done so without your knowledge—because then you can forget about probable cause and due process of law. The government need only make the assertion that you are engaged in "racketeering" and your property is confiscated immediately. Good luck proving a negative to get it back. As for not being held liable under tort law if you or your legitimate business does not harm someone—how naive. Wait until you have something stolen from you, or you legitimately sell something perfectly legal to someone, and he resells it, and then someone steals it from that person. The injury caused by its misuse is *your fault!*

Should you punch someone while calling him a son of a bitch, you have committed the crime of assault and battery under the laws of the state in which the punching took place, but should you punch him while calling him a black, white, Jew, Catholic, Protestant, Italian, Irish, *[fill in your prejudice here]* son of a bitch, you have committed a federal "hate crime," for which you will receive extra punishment. When I was in the FBI and someone came in to complain about something that was reprehensible but not against any known criminal statute, and the complainant would insist that we do something, *anything,* we would carefully explain that Congress had not yet passed the Federal Son of a Bitch Act. Well, now it has.

Indeed, it is startling to realize how much the federal government is encroaching on our freedoms. The latest United States Government Manual lists more than five hundred different federal agencies having thousands and thousands of federal bureaucrats. You and I are being taxed to pay their salaries, all so they can regulate our lives in countless ways.

How did this happen to us?

———————

Perhaps above all else, we are losing our liberties because so many Americans today are ignorant of what made this nation so extraordinary. Simply put, too many Americans don't understand the blessings our Founders bequeathed to us.

If we don't even know what a free country is, we can't possibly expect to understand when our freedoms are being violated.

So here's a definition: Liberty is the state or fact of living as a free person; individual liberty means being free from external restraint in the exercise of natural rights and acquired rights. Natural rights are those necessary for the fulfillment of man's human nature or, if you will, his human existential ends—the attainment of his best self. Acquired rights are those that are gained via legislation—such as a publicly subsidized college education for veterans.

Our forefathers understood this. They fled the strong central governments of Europe and the abuse, if not outright denial, of individual rights. To win their freedom and sovereignty, the original thirteen colonies revolted. Yet after securing independence, our Founders knew that the former colonies must remain ever vigilant if they wished to preserve the freedom for which they had fought. Each state could not go it alone on certain matters, particularly when it came to military defense. To that end the Founders reluctantly created a central government. But so deep was their fear of centralized authority that they determined to create a weak national government that would have the power to do *only* that which its constituent sovereign states could not do effectively.

Our Constitution is remarkable in its simplicity. Read it for yourself. You will have no difficulty at all in understanding it. We don't need lawyers interpreting and reinterpreting it. What is difficult to understand in the phrase "Congress shall make no law..."?

The only legitimate powers of the central government are those specifically enumerated in the Constitution. Still, before they would vote to ratify the new Constitution, many Founders insisted on specific guarantees of individual citizens' rights. So the Framers enacted the first ten amendments to the Constitution, which came to be known as the Bill of Rights.

The First Amendment was the most important. It guaranteed to each citizen that the federal government would never infringe on his individual right to the free exercise of religion, of speech, or of the press, his right peaceably to assemble, or his right to petition the government for a redress of grievances.

The Second Amendment guaranteed that should the federal government ever renege and violate any of the individual rights of citizens, they, the citizens, would possess the means to resist that effort and defeat it. Specifically, the amendment prohibited the federal government from infringing on the individual's right to keep and bear arms.

There followed, in the Third through Eighth Amendments, vital individual rights that citizens of the United States tend to take for granted but ought not, for these rights are eroding. The amendments protected against unreasonable searches and seizures by requiring a warrant based on probable cause; prohibited double jeopardy; affirmed that the individual could be held for a capital "or otherwise infamous" crime *only* if he had been indicted by a grand jury; declared that the individual could not be forced to testify against himself, be deprived of life, liberty, or property without due process of law, or have his private property taken for public use without just compensation; proclaimed the individual's right to counsel, to a speedy and public trial, to be informed of the nature and cause of the criminal charges against him, to confront witnesses against him, and to be able to compel witnesses in his favor; affirmed the individual's right to trial by jury; and prohibited excessive bail, excessive fines, and cruel and unusual punishments.

The importance of the Ninth and Tenth Amendments cannot be overemphasized. The Ninth Amendment made it absolutely clear that "the enumeration in the Constitution, of certain rights, shall not be construed to deny or disparage others retained by the people." In other words, the Framers of the Constitution wanted it to be absolutely clear that the people had *even more* individual rights, even if such rights were not listed explicitly in the Constitution. And the Tenth Amendment affirmed, "The powers not delegated to the United States by the Constitution, nor prohibited by it to the States, are reserved to the States respectively, or to the people." The meaning here was crystal clear: If a power is not set forth in the Constitution specifically, the federal government does not have it. It belongs to the states or to the people.

Look back at that list. It's all quite explicit, isn't it? The American people have rights, and the government can't violate them. So why is America today not the free country that the Founders established?

The first crack in the foundation the Framers built for us came with the Civil War. The war between North and South was a conflict between two theories that had been competing since America's founding—those of Thomas Hobbes and John Locke. According to the Hobbesian view, the states entering the union formed a social contract that could not be broken, no matter how the federal government violated its part of the bargain.

In contrast, the Lockean perspective was that if the federal government violated the contract terms, the constituent states could revert to the status quo ante. In the Civil War, the North imposed the Hobbesian view by force.

Subsequently, the nation generally reverted to the Framers' constitutional order and stayed that way until the administration of Woodrow Wilson. Unlike the Founders, Wilson believed in a powerful central government. The Wilson administration brought us the federal income tax, which he favored as "progressive" (that is, income-redistributive), as well as the Federal Trade Commission, which usurped the authority of the individual sovereign states to regulate business activity.

With the administration of Franklin Delano Roosevelt, all pretense of following the Constitution was abandoned. At Roosevelt's behest, the Democratic Congress passed law after law that was unconstitutional, as the U.S. Supreme Court ruled. Roosevelt then tried to pack the Supreme Court with additional justices who would vote as he wished. That end run failed, but the vote in Congress was so close that the High Court was intimidated. Thus it softened its firm stance against Roosevelt and devised a way around the Constitution that is in use to this day: a farmer growing corn on his own land to feed his own cattle for his own consumption is deemed to "affect" interstate commerce and thus is subject to federal regulation and law. This spurious interpretation of the Constitution destroyed the great concept of the Founding Fathers—to restrict the power of the central government and preserve the sovereignty of the states. With that, *anything* could come under the control of the federal government.

We have suffered loss of freedom ever since.

At the time, most people did not realize what had happened. Something was being done purportedly to alleviate their suffering under the Great Depression, and then the defining event of the twentieth century was upon them—the Second World War.

No one who did not live through it can imagine what this country was like in World War II. Though our population was more than 130 million at the start of the war, our armed forces ranked below those of Portugal and the Netherlands. Our answer to that was to put 16 million men under arms. My father was furious when told that he was too old to serve in the military, so he became an air raid warden. My maiden aunt, May, who had retired from the American Red Cross as a secretary, took the trolley car every day to travel three towns away to work in a war plant. Those war plants, all over the country, turned out tanks, ships, planes, and artillery by the thousands. The Kaiser plant alone was launching a ship a day.

I joined what was called the "Home Front." As part of the organized collection of aluminum and rubber, I went door to door to solicit contributions from housewives. I collected pots and pans and even some old rubber girdles! I sold newspapers outside a war plant, the Curtiss-Wright propeller division, which outfitted the Boeing B-17 Flying Fortress bombers.

We had a farmer come over with a horse and plow to plow up the lawn so we could grow our own vegetables, thus taking some pressure off the stores and saving precious gasoline that otherwise would have been used to deliver produce to the markets. Black clouds of smoke and oil slicks on the beach testified to the deadly efficiency of the Nazi U-boat wolf packs that lurked off our coasts. Flatbed trailers pulled up to the center of town bearing the fuselages of shot-down enemy aircraft as rallying points for the drive to have us buy war bonds and stamps to aid the war effort. To this day there remains in my mother's attic a portion of a Messerschmitt fighter I "liberated" one night.

In short, all of us—the 16 million fighting men as well as the many millions of us on the home front—contributed in any way we could, because we knew we were fighting to protect the freedoms that had always defined America and made her great.

Sadly, we didn't realize that Hitler, Hirohito, and Mussolini weren't the only threats to our liberty.

2

AMERICANS AND THEIR GUNS

WHEN I WAS A KID, MY FATHER IMPOSED gun control on me. He wouldn't buy me one. He was too young for the First World War, too old for the Second, and, unfamiliar with guns himself, he was not about to permit his young son to have one.

Gun control didn't work for me any more than it has worked for the rest of the United States. Someone who wants a gun will always be able to get one. With nothing more than a hacksaw and a file, I made my own out of a .22-caliber rifle barrel and a BB gun. When I showed it proudly to my uncle Ray, a special agent of the FBI, he deemed it unsafe and prevailed upon my father to let him give me a proper .22-caliber single-shot Winchester bolt-action rifle, which he proceeded to teach me to use safely and accurately.

Years later, as a young FBI agent myself, I was engaged in the required monthly firearms training session with the other agents of the Indianapolis field office. It was my first office of assignment, and at twenty-seven, I was the youngest there. Perhaps because I had the lightning reflexes of the young, I was fast, very fast. But not as fast as the man whose attention I drew. He was an agent who appeared to be in his seventies, way past the age of retirement. Wayne Brantner and another man up there in age, John Paul Jeter, were legends because both were part Cherokee Indian, had grown up on the Cherokee Strip in Oklahoma, and were experienced old western lawmen gunfighters who were reputed to have killed six men each in single combat before they were recruited into the FBI to teach their skills to their fellow agents.

I was standing with a group of agents, having just fired a pistol course, followed by a twelve-gauge pump-action shotgun course, when Wayne Brantner ambled over to me and said, "You kinda sudden, boy." He was referring to my speed. The others heard him, and the nickname "Sudden" stuck. I thanked Mr. Brantner, whom I held in awe, and he said, "You want to learn how to shoot, boy?"

"Yes, *sir!*" I replied.

Mr. Brantner turned to Mr. Jeter and said, "Paul, you reckon we could teach this boy somethin' 'bout shootin'?"

"I reckon," said Jeter.

So began my *real* training in gunfighting.

The first thing Wayne Brantner did was to take away my .38 S&W Special revolver. "That's a nice toy, boy," he said. "Good for target shootin'. Y'need somethin' to kill with. Here, try this." With that he lent me his heavy, large-frame, five-inch-barreled Smith & Wesson .357 Magnum revolver and hand-tooled leather speed holster with no safety strap or retaining device of any kind. Notice that what he gave me was then the state-of-the-art, most powerful handgun in the world. There is a lesson in that alone.

THE MARK OF A FREE MAN

When they found the man they called "The Iceman" in the Italian Alps on 19 September 1991, he had been dead an estimated five thousand years. Yet he was all there, preserved perfectly by the cold, complete with his possessions. The Iceman was not the first human found in a preserved state ages after death. In Scandinavia and England, peat bogs had yielded similar remains. Examination of the bog finds showed that the dead had been slain, some by garrote, some with a hole in their heads from a puncture wound. These men had only their clothing with them. They were captives, perhaps, or criminals who had been executed. What the bog men had in common was that they were not free.

The Iceman, by contrast, was found in possession of state-of-the-art weapons. He had a six-foot longbow, the same size used by English bowmen more than four thousand years later to defeat heavily armored French knights at the Battle of Agincourt. It was a remarkably powerful weapon when one considers that the Iceman was a mere five feet two inches tall. His ammunition was fourteen arrows held in a beautiful deerskin quiver. He had an ash-handled, flint-bladed dagger and something that astounded the experts—a nearly pure-copper

Remedello-style ax, something so advanced for five thousand years ago that *National Geographic* commented, "It was as if the tomb of a medieval warrior had yielded a modern rifle."

All of which was evidence that the Iceman was a free man. Since the dawn of history, free men have been armed with the most up-to-date weapons capable of being carried by hand. Arms are the mark of a free man. The Iceman had them at the ready, daily, to protect himself, his immediate family, or his clan, tribe, city, or country from attack, and to hunt food. On occasion he employed arms to overthrow tyranny and regain freedom, and, thereafter, to prevent the loss of liberty to would-be tyrants.

Again and again, the most lucid of political commentators, right up to and including the Founding Fathers of this nation and the Framers of our Constitution, have emphasized that a free people exercises, without impediment from its rulers, the right to keep and bear arms, and that the first order of business for would-be tyrants is to disarm the people.

Aristotle, born 384 B.C., criticized a plan by Hippodamos for a society in which only one class would bear arms, pointing out that the classes without arms would become "virtually the servants of those who do possess arms." He observed that nature had equipped man to select and use a variety of weapons, as distinguished from the lower animals, which are restricted by nature to the tooth and claw with which they are born. Thus, the right to bear arms flows from the nature of man.

Aristotle was hardly alone among those in the pre-Christian world in understanding that man has an inalienable right to keep and bear arms, nor was that understanding limited to the West. In 124 B.C., the Chinese emperor Han rejected a petition from his imperial chancellor to take arms from the people: "When the ancients made the five kinds of weapons, it was not for the purpose of killing each other, but *to prevent tyranny* and to punish evil. When people lived in peace, these weapons were used to control the fierce animals and to be prepared against emergencies. If there were military affairs, then these weapons were used to set up defense and form battle arrays [emphasis added]."

One of the finest explications of man's inherent right to bear arms is that of the great orator of the Roman Republic, Cicero, born 106 B.C.:

> There exists a law, not written down anywhere, but inborn in our hearts; a law which comes to us not by training or custom or reading but by derivation and absorption and adoption from nature itself; a law which has come to us not from theory but from practice, not by instruction but by natural intuition. I refer to the law which lays it down that, if our lives are endangered by plots or violence or armed robbers or enemies, any and every method of protecting ourselves is morally right. When weapons reduce them to silence, the laws no longer expect one to await their pronouncements. For people who decide to wait for these will have to wait for justice, too—and meanwhile they must suffer injustice first. Indeed, even the wisdom of the law itself, by a sort of tacit implication, permits self-defense, because it does

not actually forbid men to kill; what it does, instead, is to forbid the bearing of weapons with the intention to kill. When, therefore, an inquiry passes beyond the mere question of the weapon and starts to consider the motive, a man who has used arms in self-defense is not regarded as having carried them with a homicidal aim.

Cicero went on to say, "Civilized people are taught by logic, barbarians by necessity, communities by tradition; and the lesson is inculcated even in wild beasts by nature itself. They learn that they have to defend their own bodies and persons and lives from violence of any and every kind by all means within their power."

It doesn't get much clearer than that.

One of the greatest historians the world has ever known was the Roman Titus Livius, known as Livy, born 59 B.C. When Niccolò Machiavelli, 1,600 years later, sought to disguise thoughts that were dangerous to express, he used the pretext of commenting on the first 10 of the 142 books of Livy's *History of Rome.* That is how significant the work was and continues to be. Here is what Livy had to say on the right to bear arms: "Formerly, the right to bear arms had belonged solely to the patricians [the nobility]. Now plebeians [the common people] were given a place in the army, which was to be reclassified according to every man's property, i.e., his ability *to provide himself* a more or less complete equipment for the field.... [All the citizens] capable of bearing arms were required to provide [their own swords, spears, and other armor] [emphasis in the original]."

The Roman poet Ovid, born 43 B.C., stated unequivocally, "The law allows arms to be taken against an armed foe."

Which brings us to the central figure in the history of man, Jesus. What had the Prince of Peace to say on the subject? Consult the Book of Luke, Chapter 22, verses 35 through 38, relating the events leading up to His betrayal and execution:

> He said to them, "When I sent you out barefoot without purse or pack, were you ever short of anything?" "No," they answered. "It is different now," he said; "whoever has a purse had better take it with him, and his pack too; and if he has no sword, let him sell his cloak to buy one. For Scripture says, 'And he was counted among the outlaws,' and these, I tell you, must find fulfillment in me; indeed, all that is written of me is being fulfilled."
>
> "Look, Lord," they said, "we have two swords here." "Enough, enough!" he replied.

The Founding Fathers of our nation, the Framers of our Constitution, knew all this. They were highly educated men and learned in the history of Western civilization. As former English colonials, they were, of course, particularly aware of the history of England, a history that included a king's attempt at gun control which reads like recent acts of Congress—and which cost that king his head. Those who believed in God understood that the right of the individual to keep and bear arms is a God-given right—a *moral obligation,* in fact, because God, having given us our lives and blessed the unions that resulted in our families, holds us accountable for preserving those lives. Even those Founding Fathers who did not believe in God understood the right of the individual to keep and bear arms to be an inalienable natural right. All of the Framers of the Constitution understood, therefore, that the right of individuals to keep and bear arms preexisted, and existed independently of, any government they could or would create. Indeed, it was a part of the English common law (which at one time *required* British subjects to keep and bear arms for the security of the realm). The colonists were enraged when, during Bacon's Rebellion of 1676, gun control was imposed upon them, considering it a violation of one of their fundamental rights.

Thus, Richard Henry Lee, a driving force behind the Bill of Rights, said, "To preserve liberty, it is essential that the whole body of the people always possess arms, and be taught alike, especially when young, how to use them." Patrick Henry of Virginia, he of "give me liberty or give me death" fame, who opposed the Constitution, said, "The great object is, that every man be armed.... Everyone who is able may have a gun." James Madison, in *The Federalist* No. 46, excoriated the European governments that were "afraid to trust the people with arms" and stressed "the advantage of being armed, which the Americans possess over the people of almost every other nation."

As we have seen, many Founders fought to ensure that the new Constitution provided specific guarantees of individual citizens' rights, and it is no accident that in what we now know as the Bill of Rights the Framers clearly documented the right to bear arms. The Second Amendment states that "A well-regulated

Militia, being necessary to the security of a free State, the right of the people to keep and bear arms, shall not be infringed."

One question that has been raised is, Who are the militia? The Constitution contains no definition, but George Mason of Virginia answered that directly in 1788: "Who are the Militia? They consist now of the whole people." The spirit of his definition was followed in the first Militia Act of 8 May 1792, which required enrollment of most able-bodied white males between the ages of seventeen and forty-five. Even now, Congress defines the militia (in 10 U.S. Code Section 311) to include almost all men between the ages of seventeen and forty-five. In contemporary America, some claim that "militia" refers to the state and national guards, but the last I heard, all men between the ages of seventeen and forty-five were *not* members of the National Guard, nor any state guard.

There also has been a lot of twaddle bandied about in recent years that the prefatory words "A well-regulated Militia, being necessary to the security of a free State..." somehow indicate that "the right of the people to keep and bear arms" is not an individual right, as in the First and Fourth Amendments, but a "collective" right. Nothing could be more false. As Roy Copperud, author of *American Usage and Style: The Consensus* and a member of the *American Heritage Dictionary* usage panel, has pointed out:

The words "A well-regulated militia, being necessary to the security of a free state..." constitute a present participle, rather than a clause. It is used as an adjective, modifying "militia," which is followed by the main clause of the sentence (subject "the right," verb "shall"). The right to keep and bear arms is asserted as essential for maintaining a militia.... The sentence does not restrict the right to keep and bear arms, nor does it state or imply possession of the right elsewhere by others than the people; it simply makes a positive statement with respect to the right of the people.... The right to keep and bear arms is not said by the amendment to depend on the existence of a militia. No condition is stated or implied as to the relation of the right to keep and bear arms and to the necessity of a well-regulated militia as requisite to the security of a free state. *The right to keep and bear arms is deemed unconditional by the entire sentence* [emphasis added].

The Framers were highly educated men and masters of the English language; they knew exactly what they were saying.

The Real Reasons for Gun Control

If, historically and grammatically, I am stating the obvious when I say that the right of the people to keep and bear arms is an individual right which the Second Amendment forbids the federal government to infringe, whence comes gun control? It comes from plain, simple, and ugly racism, that's where. It is one more noxious legacy of slavery.

For example, my home state of Maryland, while still a colony, in its Acts of 1715 stated:

> That no Negro or other slave within this province shall be permitted to carry any gun, or any other offensive weapon, from off their master's land, without a license from their said master; and if any Negro or other slave shall presume to do so, he shall be liable to be carried before a justice of the peace, and be whipped, and his gun or other offensive weapon shall be forfeited to him that shall seize the same and carry such Negro so offending before a justice of the peace.

In 1840, North Carolina enacted a statute that provided:

> That if any free Negro, mulatto, or free person of color, shall wear or carry about his or her person, or keep in his or her house, any shot gun, musket, rifle, pistol, sword, dagger or bowie-knife, unless he or she shall have obtained a license therefore for the Court of Common Pleas and Quarter Sessions of his or her county, within one year preceding the wearing, keeping or carrying thereof, he or she shall be guilty of a misdemeanor, and may be indicted therefore.

This in spite of the fact that the 1776 North Carolina Constitution declared that "the people have a right to bear arms."

Then there is the Supreme Court's notorious *Dred Scott* decision (1857), which declared black people to be chattel, like domestic animals, and argued that to recognize "persons of the Negro race ... as citizens in any one State of the Union" would be to confer the rights of American citizenship on them. That, Chief Justice Roger Taney wrote in his opinion, would allow blacks the right to "go where they pleased at every hour of the day or night without molestation; ... the full liberty of speech; ... [the right] to hold public meetings upon political affairs, *and to keep and carry arms wherever they went* [emphasis added]." "And all of this," the chief justice wrote, would inevitably produce "discontent and insubordination among [blacks], ... endangering the peace and safety of the State."

Of course, black people are not the only minority that worries the gun controllers. In 1920, the Ohio Supreme Court received the appeal of a Mexican convicted of carrying a concealed handgun while he was in his own home, asleep, in bed. *The court upheld the conviction!* But listen to the dissent of Justice Wannamaker: "I desire to give some special attention to some of the authorities cited, supreme court decisions from Alabama, Georgia, Arkansas, Kentucky, and one or two inferior court decisions from New York, which were given in support of the doctrines upheld by this court. The southern states have very largely furnished the precedents. It is only necessary to observe that the race issue there has extremely intensified a decisive purpose to entirely disarm the negro, and that this policy is evident upon reading the opinions."

It is not a coincidence that Congress passed the Gun Control Act of 1968 in the wake of the black rioting that erupted following the assassination of Dr. Martin Luther King Jr. Whites were terrified as they watched whole sections of their cities engulfed in flames and buildings being looted. Blacks were terrified, too, many putting up makeshift signs saying "Black Owned" in an effort to spare the small businesses upon which their livelihoods depended. But blacks were not in a position to react with legislation—whites were. Senator Thomas Dodd of Connecticut had the 1938 German gun-control law that the Nazis used so effectively to disarm the Jews translated into English and then used it as the basis of the Gun Control Act of 1968, as Jay Simkin and Aaron Zelman showed in their book *"Gun Control": Gateway to Tyranny.* Of course, the 1968 act didn't name blacks as its object any more than the Nazi law of thirty years before had named Jews.

Jews weren't fooled in 1938, and blacks weren't fooled in 1968. Listen to Roy Innis, director of the Congress of Racial Equality:

> Any intent to ban the sale of "Saturday night specials" needs to be examined within a proper historical perspective. "Niggertown Saturday night specials" was a term used by racists in the South to describe pot metal guns used by blacks for protection. Today, the "Niggertown" has been dropped, but for those of us who know the meaning of the term, it's no less hurtful and offensive.

In the past, because of the South and its racist gun-control laws, blacks were confined to the sub-rosa market of the inexpensive, dangerous, so-called "Saturday night specials" to obtain means of protection. Today, in many crime-ridden minority communities, that need still exists. History teaches that racism creeps into law under good intentions. Attempts to ban handguns that are inexpensive (but safe) are directly aimed at minority gun ownership. It's more useful to educate all citizens about firearms safety.

In his characteristically blunt (but very perceptive) style, Eldridge Cleaver said of the Gun Control Act of 1968, "Some very interesting laws are being passed. They don't name me; they don't say take the guns away from the niggers. They say that the people will no longer be allowed to have guns. They don't pass these rules and regulations specifically for black people; they have to pass them in a way that will take in everybody."

Cleaver was right. But how can this happen so easily?

There exists in this country an elite that believes itself entitled to tell the rest of us what we may and may not do—for our own good, of course. These left-of-center, Ivy-educated molders of public opinion are concentrated in the mass news media, the entertainment business, academia, the pundit corps, and the legislative, judicial, and administrative government bureaucracies. Call it the divine right of policy wonks. These people feed on the great American middle class, who do the actual work of this country and make it all happen. They bleed us with an income tax rate not seen since we were fighting for our lives in the middle of World War II; they charge us top dollar at the box office for movies that assail and undermine the values we are attempting to inculcate in our children; they charge more and more for a constantly degraded higher education for which most of us arrive unprepared because of an even more degraded elementary and secondary school education . . . for which they want more and more money.

I believe it has occurred to these self-anointed "betters" that, at some point, we the people are likely to say "Enough!" and at that point, the thought of 100 million Americans armed with 230 million firearms is positively terrifying.

So what to do? The elite musters all of its assets. Seventy-five thousand hapless females, following the nitwit Rosie O'Donnell, become the "Million Mom March" against firearms ownership. Moreover, the Centers for Disease Control and Prevention (death by firearm a disease?) claims that firearms are a significant cause of death for children. The gullible believe it. But look at the facts. First, the Centers for Disease Control defines as "children" all those aged nineteen and under—despite the fact that the law states one becomes an emancipated adult at age eighteen, and despite the fact that we treat fourteen-year-olds as adults in our justice system and prosecute them accordingly. In reality, most gun-related deaths among fifteen- to nineteen-year-olds are the result of inner-city gang and drug wars. How many accidental deaths among children fourteen and under were the result of firearms? In 1998 (the latest data as of this writing), the figure was 121. So are guns a "significant" cause of death among children? To answer that question, consider other figures for accidental deaths in the same age group: 2,566 children died in automobile accidents, 1,003 died from drowning, 661 from accidental suffocation, and 608 from accidental burns. But the media won't tell you that.

YOUR LIBERTY IS NO LOOPHOLE

The elite tell you that more guns in the hands of the populace results in more crime. The opposite is true. The experiences of both Great Britain and Australia are enlightening. When, as the result of demands to "do something" after an individual committed a mass killing using firearms, each nation abolished the right of individuals to possess guns, the violent crime rate shot upward. The reason is that, in both countries, the criminals still have no difficulty being armed, while the law-abiding are left defenseless. In the four years after Great Britain implemented its gun ban, gun crime rose by 40 percent. By the year 2000, the overall crime rate in England and Wales was 60 percent higher than the crime rate in the United States. In Australia, armed robberies, after having decreased steadily for twenty-five years, rose by 44 percent in just the first year under the new gun laws. Overall, since Australia's gun ban went into effect, assaults have risen by 24 percent and kidnappings by 43 percent.

Although one would never know it through the media, armed citizens in the United States *prevent* crime. Armed citizens thwart criminals 2.5 million times a year, and citizens shoot and kill twice as many criminals as the police do every year. In those states where concealed-carry laws have been passed, there has been a dramatic drop in violent crime. Indeed, as far back as 1979, the Carter Justice Department released figures showing that of 32,000 attempted rapes, 32 percent were actually committed, but only 3 percent were successful when the woman was armed.

Remember that the next time the media, the politicians, the college professors, and the "Beautiful People" tell you that their proposed new gun-control law is just to "close another loop-hole." You tell them that your right to keep and bear arms is God-given, inalienable, and protected by the Constitution; that we have more than twenty thousand gun-control laws on the books now, of which few are constitutional; and that *your liberty is no loophole!*

3

EDUCATION

FROM TIME TO TIME, MY RADIO LISTENERS remark on my ability to converse intelligently with the wide range of guests I have on the air. On the program, I regularly talk to authors about their books, which cover everything from astrophysics to xenophobia. Other guests include classical musical artists, popular-culture icons, sports legends, motion picture stars, powerful political figures, high-ranking military officers, opinion makers, historians, professors, astronauts, and automobile mechanics.

How do I manage to discuss such a wide range of topics with such an array of individuals? First, I have a large frame of reference. I experienced 70 percent of the history of the twentieth century—and, in fact, made some of it. Over the years, I have been an Army officer, FBI special agent, prosecutor, defense and appellant counsel, defendant, convict, prisoner, Treasury official, White House aide, author, lecturer, actor, and radio broadcaster.

One factor, however, is paramount: education. I am the beneficiary of a superb education, because my parents knew how important my schooling was.

My father, a brilliant man, spent much of his youth in poverty. He was a superb athlete who won countless medals at track and field meets; he was such a talented baseball player that the legendary John McGraw asked him to try out for the New York Giants. My father declined. Why? Because he knew that *education* was the better and more reliable ticket out of poverty. Accordingly, while working on the docks at a time when one held a job by fighting with a cargo hook, he sat for examinations to win scholarships first to a fine Benedictine college preparatory school in New Jersey, St. Benedict's Prep, and then to what is still the country's finest Jesuit college of arts and sciences, Fordham, in New York City. He went on to become the best lawyer in the United States in his specialty of trademarks and unfair competition.

My mother taught me to read before I was in the first grade, using the pure phonics method (the only one that works). I think it was so that she wouldn't have to continue to read to me, because in the days before laborsaving appliances, and with a baby girl to care for also, she was too busy.

My first adult book, read at age eight, was *Swiss Family Robinson*. I devoured it, and when I was finished, my mother found me crying and asked me why. "Because it's over," I sobbed. That was the measure of the delight that book afforded me.

It was the Great Depression and there was little money. My reward for being a good boy was a Saturday trip to the local library and the privilege of selecting my own books for reading during the week.

I read Tennyson's *Idylls of the King,* which first acquainted me with the Arthurian legend. There followed Stevenson's *Treasure Island;* Cooper's *Last of the Mohicans;* Dumas's *Count of Monte Cristo;* Twain's *Tom Sawyer, A Connecticut Yankee in King Arthur's Court,* and *Huckleberry Finn,* with its incredibly funny tale of the freeing of Jim from imprisonment in the shed, to appreciate which one had to be familiar with *The Count of Monte Cristo* (and note, the rustic Tom Sawyer was familiar with it—how many big-city high school students today can say the same?); L. Frank Baum's *Oz* series (I knew the story before I saw the first run of the movie in 1939, and I can say the same for Margaret Mitchell's *Gone With the Wind*); Sir Walter Scott's *Ivanhoe* (in the original excellent, but difficult, English). I breezed through Edgar Rice Burroughs's *Tarzan* series, as well as Booth Tarkington's *Penrod* and *Penrod Jashber,* and the hilarious *Seventeen.* I read serious science books like *By Rocket to the Moon,* which told of the Goddard efforts long before anyone had ever heard of Wernher von Braun; nonserious science fiction by H. G. Wells; and British crime novels by Leslie Charteris (the *Saint* series), Agatha Christie, and Arthur Conan Doyle (a great favorite). By age thirteen, I had read all of Shakespeare's plays and poetry, some of the latter affecting me quite erotically. I even recall "borrowing" my mother's copy of Daphne du Maurier's *Rebecca.*

In the summer, when there was no school, and when I was ill, I read with such speed and proficiency that by finishing under the covers with a flashlight, I was able to read a simple book (like one of the *Tarzan* series) in a day. I was myopic by age sixteen.

I read the *Book of Knowledge* volumes, then the *Encyclopedia Britannica* (skipping, I must confess, the biographies of many nineteenth-century British politicians). Fortunately, in my youth there was no television to stunt my imagination; reading, and the few radio programs (the "theater of the mind") that I was permitted to listen to, stimulated it constantly.

The relentless reading, especially of the beautiful prose of English and Scottish authors, so ingrained in me a knowledge of correct English grammar—syntax, agreement, etc.—that I could recognize error instantly, even before I learned in school what rule it was that was being violated. It was as if I had developed perfect pitch for the music of the English language. All this before I read in school the classics of the Brontës, Henry James, Byron, and in my opinion the greatest master of the language, Milton. I read Chaucer in college, but not before first taking a course in Middle English so I could read him in the original.

Not long ago, I showed one of my old textbooks to a public high school teacher. "That's graduate-level stuff" was his reaction. The book was one I used in my junior year in prep school in 1946. Clearly, the quality and rigor of American education are moving in the wrong direction.

My father sent me to the same schools he had attended. So I had the privilege to be taught by Benedictine monks (some, German refugees who were given asylum in monasteries in the United States during World War II) and Jesuit priests, who had to acquire the functional equivalent of three Ph.D.s during sixteen years of training before ordination. My father had studied

Latin; Greek; German; ancient, modern, and American history; physics; organic and inorganic chemistry; algebra; plane and solid geometry; and trigonometry—and his grades were in the highest 90s out of 100. I know, because he showed me his report cards and made the message clear: I was expected to do just as well or better. While I received very high grades, I bested my father only once—I received a 99 in plane geometry. I would have received 100, but "only God is perfect."

I consider myself fortunate to have received such a fine education. But as we know all too well, America's schools are not what they once were. I have carefully studied the issue of education through the years, and I know what plagues our schools.

I hasten to add that I have great respect for our teachers, because I know just how hard it is to educate children properly. My wife, Frances, was a teacher in the tough public schools of northeast Washington, D.C. Her mother was a teacher. Her aunts Anne and Etta were teachers. My daughter-in-law is a teacher. My father was a teacher before he became a lawyer. My son Tom, a former Marine captain of infantry, has also taught school. He told me it is every bit as tough as being a U.S. Marine, and in many respects, tougher. Until you stand in front of a class-room with thirty children whose futures are entrusted to you, you cannot possibly know how hard a job it is. Teachers—the good ones—deserve our gratitude and our respect, as well as good pay.

The problem is that on the whole American education just does not deliver anymore.

THE EDUCATION SYSTEM: AN ASSAULT ON LIBERTY

As parents and citizens, we all have a moral obligation to educate our children. My parents understood that. Each one of us benefits when children grow up to be productive citizens. What makes America so special is that we are free and everybody has an opportunity to pursue happiness and build a productive life. But the American Dream is simply unattainable to a child who is denied a quality education. The promise of America is simple, and beautiful: Come to these shores legally; work yourself to exhaustion in a free-enterprise system that rewards hard workers and smart calculated-risk takers; educate your children so that they can rise in the world's greatest meritocracy.

An uneducated person cannot succeed in this environment. Even many minimum-wage jobs require some ability to read. Several major automobile manufacturers report that they turn away more than a third of the applicants for assembly-line jobs because they are functionally illiterate. I will never forget, back in my time working in the Nixon administration, when I was walking to the White House one day and an obviously frustrated courier asked me if I knew where Connecticut Avenue was. I looked up. Not five yards from where we stood was a green street sign on which was printed "CONNECTICUT." Unfortunately, the young man could not read the sign. Sure, someone could give him precise directions on how to get somewhere, but if anything went awry he was at the mercy of a stranger to help. It pained me to think that this man might have a family to support.

Please note, however, that when I refer to education, I am *not* talking about *training*. When I spoke of my own education, I did not mention Fordham Law School or the New York University Graduate School of Law, for learning the skills of a lawyer—or a surgeon or an electrician or a pipe fitter or an accountant—is mere training. *Education* is learning how to think critically and absorbing mankind's accumulated wisdom and culture. It is the foundation for everything else, period.

When it comes to restoring and preserving our freedom, education is essential. A major reason that so many Americans do not realize their liberties are slipping from their grasp is that they are simply unaware of the tyranny our forefathers rebelled against. The only way to understand why so many strong souls risked everything, including their lives, to climb aboard leaking wooden ships and cross the Atlantic for a mere chance at building a better life is to know the failings of their governments. The tyranny of such governments spawned the great works of Hobbes, Locke, and Rousseau, which inspired the learned men who conceived of the American experiment. Those men, too, had suffered under tyranny. Once the colonies became established, the British monarch pressed the colonists for more and more of their hard-earned wealth in the form of taxes and restrictions on their trading routes, all without affording them the one thing they valued most: a say in the conduct of their own government. If one does not know this history, one can have no sense of why our Founders pledged their lives, their fortunes, and their sacred honor to gamble for freedom—by taking on, and defeating, the eighteenth century's leading superpower.

Unfamiliar with this history, Americans sit by and watch politicians in Washington chip away at our individual liberties. Indeed, without education, one does not even know what liberty is. In a country such as ours, the people are sovereign and must govern themselves. We do so by expressing our will at the ballot box at regular intervals. Education enables us to understand the issues and express ideas on how best to solve societal problems. It also allows us to evaluate candidates, their proposals, and the veracity of their assertions. Even in the age of electronic media, one must not only be literate but also have a certain base-level liberal education to engage fully in our democracy. The uneducated are far more vulnerable to manipulation by politicians and thus are less capable of self-governing. They are not truly free.

THE PROBLEMS

Today, the majority of our children are receiving an inferior education. The Third International Mathematics and Science Study (TIMSS), released in 1996, found that the performance of American students was *below average* in math and just a little above average in science, and was *significantly* behind the performances of students from countries such as Singapore, Korea, Japan, and Hungary. In a follow-up study conducted in 1999, the results were about the same—and probably would have been much worse had the study not excluded several European nations along with India and China. Even more disturbing was a trend noted in the original TIMSS: American fourth graders were above average in math and science, but our eighth graders were just average—and our twelfth graders were near the bottom.

That will not do! Other countries would like to take our power and economic wealth away from us, so America must be ever ready to protect its position in the world and the standard of living for which so many have fought so hard. That means having the best minds to make sure we are ahead in the global marketplace as well as on the battlefield. As a great nation, we can and must address this situation.

So what is the problem? There are lots of problems, to be sure, but the single biggest mistake American schools have made is that they have forgotten the ground rule of educational success: competition is king.

Today's educrats recoil from the very idea of competition. Trained in liberal teachers colleges that ignore the basics of how to teach reading, writing, and arithmetic in order to focus on such nonsense as "teaching theory," "conflict resolution," methods for building and maintaining self-esteem in failing students, and celebrating ethnic diversity, they have forgotten everything that once made America's education system the envy of the world. They need a refresher course in American history. America was always geared to producing winners. Competing and winning were part of the psychology of being an American. All citizens embraced it—rich and poor, black and white, Jew and gentile.

In my early years, children competed to win in all areas of school life—academics, sports, debating, the school band. Winning mattered. Hard work was the norm. Progress was graded and posted. Winners stood out and were recognized. Losers were encouraged to work harder to improve, or to find a niche where they could excel. Americans were realists about human strengths and weaknesses. The job was to find your strength and maximize your potential.

Nowhere was competition more intense than in gym class. Whether we were on the track, on the ball field, or in the gym, there were winners and losers. Winners had the fastest times, scored the most runs, or completed the most push-ups or sit-ups.

I was weak and sickly most of my childhood. When I was in the eighth grade at St. Aloysius Elementary School, I weighed a mere 120 pounds. I desperately wanted to play on the baseball team, but it seemed I had no prayer of making it. Yet I saw an opportunity to exercise the will to compete that my parents had instilled in me. All the other kids wanted to play pitcher, short-stop, or first base. Nobody wanted to play catcher for fear of being hit in the head by a fastball or being bowled over at home plate. (We didn't have the modern, ultraprotective catcher's equipment.) There was my chance. The only way to deal with the fear of being knocked over was to get behind the plate and be knocked over. So that's what I did. Whether I got hit in the head with a bat or bowled over at the plate, I kept at it—and with that attitude and commitment, I made the team.

What my parents taught me, and what the educationists fail to recognize, is that these competitions are not pointless exer-cises. Life is a competition, and I learned from an early age how to prepare myself and work hard to achieve what I wanted. In those days, winners took joy in winning. Losers took it hard. If you didn't win, you were determined to work harder and win the next time. We learned to push ourselves, to test our limits in an exercise of personal exploration. My father showed me his old report cards and expected me to match his academic performance for a simple but important reason: he was setting goals for me—difficult goals that would require hard work and dedication to achieve.

Generation after generation of Americans grew up this way—pushed in school to work hard, to compete, to test themselves, to use their special gifts, whatever those might be. And win we did: America made the best cars and planes, produced world-class steel, even formed the world's greatest military to defeat Hitler's Third Reich and Hirohito's Imperial Japan.

Winning: what an abominable idea! At least, that is what today's educationists would have us think. A teacher in liberal Takoma Park, Maryland, sums up today's thinking. He discourages competition, he says, because "I don't think kids need to deal with competition." Oh? Just wait until they graduate!

Instead of emphasizing results—which would require students to work hard and would show (gasp) that some were achieving more than others—American schools now focus on dumbing everything down so students can "feel good" about themselves. This practice has reached absurd levels. Consider gym class, formerly the realm of the stiffest competition among students. Today kids experience the new, politically correct system of "physical education." Old standbys like dodgeball, with its winners and losers, are out. For example, Fairfax County, Virginia, an affluent suburb of Washington, D.C., adopted a new physical education curriculum focusing on "health maintenance" and discouraging students from competing. One school, Oak View Elementary, had been recognized thirteen times for its outstanding performances on the President's Physical Fitness Test, in which students across the nation compete in a long-distance run, a fifty-yard sprint, pull-ups, sit-ups, and more. But Oak View stopped emphasizing the national competition and instituted this "New PE." Apparently the school's record of achievement was a source not of pride but of shame.

The rampant grade inflation that exists in our schools today is another example of the misguided attempt to boost self-esteem and negate competition. Students now receive higher grades than their predecessors did without a corresponding rise in academic achievement. And this is a problem throughout the entire education system, even (or perhaps especially) at our most prestigious universities. Two-thirds of Harvard Law School students now graduate with honors. Ninety percent of letter grades at Stanford are now B or higher.

I know a young man who attends a public high school in suburban Dallas. He has an 87 average (out of 100)—a solid B-plus—but he is not in the top 50 percent of his class of some eight hundred students. When more than half the class has over a B-plus average, what does this do to the C, which is meant to represent *average* work? Today's feel-good educrats believe *everyone* should be above average, but by lowering standards so far they have created a situation in which neither a high school diploma nor admittance into college has any meaning in terms of quality.

Maybe all this fear of competition comes from the very government that runs our public schools—and which, we all know, is so averse to competition from the free market. In effect, the government has a monopoly on the education marketplace for poor and middle-class American children, whose parents cannot afford to send them to private schools. And it has been well documented how ineffective the federal government is when it comes to running our schools. Did you realize that the federal Department of Education spends upward of *$55 billion* per year (which is more than double its annual budget as recently as 1997), but of that, only a small fraction ever reaches our kids' classrooms? The very idea that bureaucrats in Washington know what is best for a school district in Alaska—or Florida or New Mexico or Maine—is absurd, and it is even more absurd to force a child to attend a public school that doesn't meet his needs. *All* parents should be given the choice of where to send their kids to school—through charter schools, vouchers, and tax credits. The bottom line is that parents deserve the freedom to choose what is best for their child. The increased competition in the marketplace will benefit *all* children.

The problem is not just in the schools or with the government, however. Education is, first and foremost, a parental responsibility, and too often parents do not give the proper commitment to education. I am grateful that my parents valued education so highly and stressed its importance to me. They remind me of the situation in South Korea, where many middle-class parents spend up to 50 percent of their take-home pay on private tutors to supplement their children's education. That gives a child a lot more one-on-one academic instruction, of course, but more important, it shows the child that his parents value education and are willing to undergo tremendous financial hardship for his long-term benefit. *That* builds self-esteem! It also pushes the child to work hard in school—and to become educated means years of hard work and self-discipline. Americans who are upset at the state of America's schools need to look inward. What is more valuable, a thirty-five-inch television set with the latest DVD player or three hours a week of one-on-one instruction for your child? As parents, we have to make sacrifices to give our kids the best possible start in life.

America was built on a culture of sacrifice, hard work, and moral courage. That is what it takes to succeed in school and in life. Generation after generation of American immigrants from all over the world motivated their children to master English and other subjects in school so they could reap the benefits of the American Dream. Today's intelligent American immigrants do the same thing. The ignorant are increasingly deceived into banding together to resist, rather than achieve, assimilation, especially in culture and language. Those who would exploit them politically encourage this self-defeating attitude, and it is no help that corporate and municipal America panders to their ignorance of English by offering automatic teller machines and government application forms in foreign languages.

THE PREDICTABLE EFFECTS

So what happens when we have schools controlled by bureaucrats in Washington, teachers who shy away from "dealing with competition," and parents who are not committed enough to their children's education? Well, we get the failed American education system, of course.

We have seen that our schools began worsening as this country experienced a cultural shift away from the emphasis on competition and achievement. The results are predictable, and dreadful. Unfortunately, while the majority of our teachers are talented, dedicated men and women whom we are blessed to have serving our children, many have not mastered the very subjects they are charged with teaching. Lots of states require public school teachers to spend two years learning useless, even harmful, educationist theories (e.g., the "whole language" method of reading instruction) and not enough of the fundamentals of phonics-based reading, or writing according to the rules of grammar, or calculation, or using such tools as memorized "times tables," or the history of Western civilization and the United States, or basic geography.

"Teachers" who are not grounded in the subjects they teach should be removed from the system. (After all, one does not instruct children in "teaching theory.") So why aren't they? Because the powerful teachers' unions fight to make sure there is no real accountability. For years, communities have been trying to initiate teacher testing and merit pay for exceptional teachers, but they are fought every step of the way.

For example, while serving as chancellor of Boston University, the conservative Democrat John Silber witnessed how some of the best public school students in Massachusetts failed when they arrived on campus each fall. "The system of institutions preparing persons to become public school teachers," he announced, "is an utter failure and badly in need of radical reform or being shut down." Silber decided to act, agreeing to serve on Massachusetts's Board of Education. Under Silber's leadership, the board took dramatic steps to improve the quality of teachers, such as offering twenty-thousand-dollar bonuses to draw some of the most able teachers to Massachusetts and requiring each teacher in the school system to take a competency exam.

Silber and the parents should have known something was amiss when the teachers' union fought against the test so fiercely. But even the most cynical could not have foreseen the results of the competency test. *Fifty-nine percent* of the soon-to-be public school teachers flunked. The teachers colleges were saying that their graduates knew how to teach, but the test results said that they did not know anything *to* teach. Nevertheless, most of those who flunked thought they could be good teachers anyway. I guess one does not have to know, say, the rules of grammar to motivate and inspire others to learn them. But imagine what happens when a student asks, "If I want to write two independent clauses to express an idea, must I write two sentences separated by a period, or may I separate them with a coordinate conjunction and a comma?" The response, courtesy of the composition teacher who does not know the fundamentals: "Huh? Uh...go look it up. It's in your book. Feel good about yourself. Be the best you can be!" This is the theory of education employed by Professor Harold Hill in *The Music Man:* he didn't need to know how to read or play music as long as he could hum a tune into the instruments and make the children *believe* they could play them.

You might think this is as bad as it gets, but you would be wrong. Massachusetts decided to *lower* the standards to allow 260 of the 1,250 who had flunked the test to become teachers anyway! Now there is quite a lesson: If you do not like the results of the test, why, change the test. It must be too hard to teach reading, writing, and calculating to young men and women who want to teach those subjects themselves.

The citizens of Massachusetts had the good sense to be outraged. Fortunately, they created enough public pressure to keep those 260 flunkers out of the public schools and to force the education commissioner to resign. So it seems there *is* some public accountability in Massachusetts, its citizens' tendency to elect anyone named Kennedy notwithstanding.

Sadly, it was a rare victory for our schools and our children. Public schools remain a breeding ground for academic failure. It is as if they exist to provide jobs for teachers and administrators, not to educate our children so they can go out into the world and achieve. As a result of the misguided educrats, college students across the country now spend much of the first two years in remedial classes learning what students were once taught in high school. In the summer of 1997, the City University of New York found itself in court waiting to learn if college seniors who had failed their English proficiency examination would be allowed to graduate anyway. How could there be two sides to this issue? The question should have been, Why were these students ever admitted to the once proud CUNY in the first place?

Despite such depressing stories, however, we should not lose hope. We have the ability to succeed as a nation that values education if we support the many innovative Americans who are willing to work hard to improve our schools. We have some powerful assets. America's schools, both public and private, still have many able and dedicated teachers. Breaking the government monopoly on public schools would permit much-needed innovation in teaching methods and curricula. That is why every American should stand behind school choice, local control of schools (one-size-fits-all solutions from politicians and bureaucrats in Washington do not work for our kids), and a curriculum that teaches the basics—reading, mathematics, the physical sciences, history, expository prose, geography, philosophy, logic—and not political correctness, self-esteem building, and other nonsense.

But many Americans are understandably frustrated with the intractable teachers' unions and the inability to make immediate changes to our education system. True enough, as much as we advocate innovations like school choice, these are ultimately policy matters that rest in the hands of politicians. And even the most involved parents do not have absolute authority over their child's curriculum.

There is plenty that you can do, however.

TAKE CHARGE

The lesson here is to be an active parent and fight for your child's education. Don't just sit back and take whatever education the public schools in your neighborhood are offering. If your state has not yet enacted school-choice laws, you can investigate the school system in your area to determine the sort of education your child will receive there.

Ideally you will choose the neighborhood in which you will raise your children only after you have investigated the school system. If you have the means, buy a home in an area that has excellent schools and, more important, is filled with families that value education highly. Too many students succumb to peer pressure from kids who think it is "cool" to dress poorly, use drugs, and fail in school. Why subject your child to that? Surround him with children whose parents feel the same about education as you do.

The easiest way to do this is to send your child to a private school, for parents who make such a significant financial commitment to their children's schooling value education highly. That makes a difference. Moreover, in a private school your child's curriculum will not be set by a group of politically correct nitwits who care only about pleasing politicians and dumbing everything down so the test results show everyone to be "equal."

Of course, countless American families, even those willing to make significant sacrifices for their children, simply cannot afford to send their kids to private school or move into neighborhoods with strong public schools. That's okay, because the most important figures in a child's education are his parents. Indeed, education begins at home, long before a child ever reaches school. So how can you educate your child?

Start at the beginning, by building as solid a foundation as you possibly can. Studies now confirm what our parents knew instinctively: the earliest years of a child's life are critical to intellectual development. A child's brain begins to develop in response to external stimuli even before birth. That means it is never too early to start preparing your child to learn.

It all starts with reading. The alphabet, phonics, and vocabulary make up the code that will unlock the great treasures of the world, the accumulated wisdom and experience of mankind, for your child (and for you). So read to your baby. There are countless books geared to infants, with few words and lots of colorful illustrations. These books are designed to provide your infant important auditory and visual stimuli that, when presented together, enhance vocabulary development and train the brain to recognize tone and word patterns.

Children learn English by hearing usage patterns over and over during the critical formative years. That is why you must be careful to check the books you read to your child, since so many children's books contain grammatical errors. In addition, it is imperative that you speak correct English to your child. In other words, *avoid all baby talk!* Before children can speak well, they are absorbing information at an incredible rate and are recognizing speech patterns. So speak to your three-year-old as you would an adult, and read him books written in correct English.

Because children absorb so much during their early years, as a parent you must closely monitor all the sensory input. Sing to your child. Check out audiotapes of traditional songs and nursery rhymes from the library. And play classical music for your child. Classical music is the auditory manifestation of higher math. It is filled with thousands of temporal patterns that all fit together. It is good for your child's brain. Just as important, classical music is not beset by the poor grammar that plagues so much popular music, be it pop, rock, hip-hop, rap, new wave, alternative, or country. You do not want your child picking up poor speaking habits that could haunt him for a lifetime. In *My Fair Lady* (the musical based on George Bernard Shaw's *Pygmalion*), Professor Henry Higgins had it right when he said, "Look at her, a prisoner of the gutter, condemned by every syllable she utters." Even the best-dressed or most distinguished-looking person will be judged ignorant or vulgar if he cannot speak correctly and articulately. Some of the dead giveaways: "Me and Bob" (for "Bob and I"); "I don't have no time" (for "I have no time"; "I don't have any time"; "I don't have time"); "They invited Sally and I" (for "They invited Sally and me").

Another essential step is to turn off the TV. I was lucky. When I was a boy there was no television, only radio. Radio, with its words and sound effects, stimulated the imagination much as reading does, and I have been the richer for it. But so many parents today rely on television as a babysitter, which is about the worst thing you can do as a parent. Watching television is a passive activity—the child watches and listens but *does* nothing. That does not stimulate the brain, which is why television is so harmful for child development. Watching TV (and motion pictures) means simply absorbing auditory and visual signals. What you see is what you get; there is no imagination required.

Television time also takes away from reading time. When we read, our imaginations take over and supply all sorts of details. That is why we are almost invariably disappointed by films based on good books we have read: nothing can compete with the human imagination—not even Hollywood, with its unlimited budgets, exotic locations, and high-tech special effects.

But if a child does not *exercise* his imagination, it will fail to develop properly—and if he does not continue to exercise it, the mind will atrophy. Don't let that happen to your child. Develop his imagination with good books and stories. Some of the greatest stories you can tell your child are part of our cultural heritage: stories from the Bible, Aesop's Fables, tales from American history, and much more. Read with your child *all the time:* in the morning, during the day, at bedtime. You never want to pressure your child to read or punish him by forcing him to read. Nor, for that matter, do you want to use reading books to or with your child as a reward. Simply put, by making reading time a regular occurrence, you will show that reading is fun. By the time your child is able to read on his own, you will probably have inculcated a lifelong habit. Ultimately books will open your child's eyes to history, culture, science, geography, politics, and so much more.

A great way to educate children is to take advantage of their natural aptitudes and curiosity. Young children are natural storytellers. Provide them with household costumes and props, paper and clay, and plenty of fresh air, and their minds will develop magically on their own. Parents can enhance this natural process. If you notice your child playing pirate, for example, you can expand on this theme by taking trips to the library to pick up books about pirates or whales or the ocean, by visiting the aquarium, or by getting an old packing box to decorate as a ship. All these things further your child's cultural repertoire and enable him to recognize connections between objects and concepts, which is so important to a higher, more abstract level of thinking.

Above all else, remember that *you* are in charge of your child's early education. Another insidious aspect of television is that it can infect your child with the cultural lessons of the Left. Those parents who use the TV as a babysitter are allowing the liberal media to raise their children. Be especially wary of public television, those much-lauded programs that purport to be educational.

When your child begins school, you must continue to play an active role in his education. Communicate to your child that you expect him to learn, and emphasize that *studying is hard work*. Set specific goals. That is what my father did in showing me his report cards and making clear that I should match his results. If your child achieves his goals, praise him—and then raise the bar higher. If there are problems, identify them immediately by conferring with your child's teacher and arranging for extra help if necessary.

Taking an active role in your child's education also means making sure he is exposed to the basics: reading, expository prose, creative writing, the physical sciences, mathematics, geography, philosophy, logic, and history. Curricula must focus on skills and facts rather than on feelings.

As a parent, you must maintain this focus throughout your child's schooling. Even when your child reaches college, at which point the student assumes primary responsibility for his own education, you should continue actively to monitor his progress. The college student should take the tough courses, and leave the courses in women's, homosexual, and popular-culture studies to others. Becoming educated means learning how to think critically, and that means taking the classic liberal arts. The student should forget about all the movies that show college as a never-ending series of beer parties. When his class-mates get drunk, pass out, and skip class, your child can take advantage of their stupidity by staying sober and working harder. Remind your kid that he is in competition with the other students for academic achievement—and that after graduation, he will be in competition in the real world.

THE LIBERALS HIJACK THE SYSTEM

The failings of the American education system are well docu-mented. And sometimes the solutions—initiatives like school choice and local control of schools—are obvious, despite what our politicians seem to think. It can be frustrating to encounter stiff resistance from liberals who think government knows best and who want to hijack our nation's schools to institute their special brand of social engineering. These are the people who want not just to offer sex education, but to teach kids *everything* there is to know about sex, and to encourage experimentation by handing out condoms in school. These are the people who have forced so many of our colleges and universities to drop required courses in Western civilization. These are the people who perpetuate racist quotas that were anathema to Dr. Martin Luther King Jr., whose most fervent desire was that all men be judged by the content of their character, not the color of their skin.

Those last two points demand further comment, for they get to the heart of what education—and this country—should be about. In recent years many colleges have watered down the emphasis on Western civilization. Rather than focusing on classic texts from Western civilization, many have added texts from Asia and Africa in an effort to make nonwhite Americans feel more included. This effort is born of the racist belief that Americans whose ancestors are not from Europe are somehow less American than those who are and that, therefore, they cannot relate to the texts and philosophies that gave birth to their American heritage.

Yet Western civilization is what binds us together as Americans. We are not bound together by race, religion, or creed. We are united by a common set of ideas: that we each have individual, inalienable rights that were bestowed on us by God; that we the people are sovereign. These ideas have sprung from Western civilization. Plato, Socrates, Aristophanes, Cicero, St. Augustine, Rousseau, Hobbes, Locke, Cervantes—these are the philosophers our Founding Fathers read, and their thinking underpinned the great American experiment.

Liberals continue to peddle cultural relativism, but Western civilization *is* superior to others, because it is based on the rights of the individual. That is why so many Americans fought and died for it. That is why so many immigrants have come, and continue to come, to these shores. We should not be afraid to proclaim that our heritage is special. Many of our universities and public schools do not even teach Western civilization anymore, or when they do, they denigrate it as oppressive or no more valuable than other civilizations. This is preposterous and endangers the long-term security of our freedom. If we do not have ideas to bind us together as a people, we have nothing to bind us together. We risk balkanization.

So-called affirmative action policies also lead to balkanization. Most colleges and universities accept some sort of federal funding and thus are bound to honor the harmful policy of using racial preferences in granting admissions. Because of racial preferences, we have undergraduates who are ill prepared to profit from the college experience, and the quality of a college degree has declined as colleges have dumbed down the curriculum and lowered grading standards and degree requirements.

In short, college admissions should be color-blind, based on merit, not on quotas, official governmental preferences, or some other politically correct consideration. Race, sex, and ethnicity are irrelevant to academic success and therefore should not be factored into the admissions equation. Of course, many high school students capable of doing college work are severely handicapped by the inadequacy of their primary and secondary educations, particularly when it comes to preparing for standardized tests such as the SAT and ACT. Thus, because the test scores of many blacks, "Hispanics," and other minorities continue to lag behind those of whites, liberals have declared war on standardized tests themselves instead of on the real threat to American education—failing public schools and the decline of families who value and nurture scholastic achievement.

Ultimately this boils down to racism—government-sanctioned racism. In November 1994, Rutgers University president Francis Lawrence defended the use of racial preferences by stating that universities should not weigh SAT scores too heavily because blacks do not have the "genetic hereditary background" to score higher. The comment predictably and justifiably caused an uproar, but Lawrence's statement merely revealed what was already obvious to the vast majority of Americans who abhor race-based quotas of any kind: those who believe that blacks, or members of any other race, are incapable of competing on a level playing field are racists, plain and simple. Such racist thinking is utterly illogical; *no* black person could score in the highest percentiles of *any* test if blacks were genetically incapable of doing so.

It is precisely this sort of backwards thinking that has so damaged our education system and, indeed, our nation. The America of my youth was not infected with such insidious ideas. This nation has abandoned what made it great in favor of unjust policies that ignore the basic promise of America: In the world's greatest meritocracy, anyone can get ahead by educating himself and working hard to succeed.

ARMING YOUR CHILDREN

Education is a tool. It can be used to enrich our lives and, in times of crisis, it can be used as a weapon to protect ourselves, our families, our country, and our freedom.

Many times in my life I have seen what a powerful weapon education can be. As I recounted in my autobiography, *Will,* my experience in federal prison taught me that "wardens had a free hand and treated the prisoners arbitrarily, paying only lip service to the statements of policy. The [Federal] Bureau of Prisons could not care less." But because I used my education, coupled with my training as a lawyer, as a weapon against the prison, I did not have to stand for this treatment.

I began preparing a lawsuit to compel the warden to obey Bureau of Prisons rules regarding solitary confinement. Any guard could throw a prisoner into solitary at will; even if the kangaroo court later found the prisoner not guilty, the man typically had already suffered for days in solitary. It gave guards enormous power over prisoners, and I was determined to strip them of it.

My opportunity arose when two other prisoners, Richard Dale Stover and Raymond S. Miley, brought an action in U.S. District Court to compel the warden to obey Bureau of Prisons policy with respect to legal mail. Stover was a bright young man but not a lawyer, so he asked me for help. With his permission I applied to the court to join our cases. Once the court granted my request to join the cases, I asked for and received permission to prosecute the case myself.

In the end, the court issued a writ of mandamus against the warden and those officials acting under his supervision. The victory rocked the prison. The hated guards had been defeated in court. In a situation in which I, as a prisoner, had seemed powerless, I used my education and my training as powerful weapons to overcome my opponent.

Parents must understand that life is filled with competition. As much as most responsible members of society try to be kind to their neighbors and help those who are down on their luck, the fact is that the world is a dangerous place. We necessarily spend our lives competing with one another for the best jobs to gain the resources necessary to establish safe and comfortable homes for our families. Once parents are exposed to and fully appreciate this fact, the next logical step is to arm their children with the most effective weaponry available for use in the competition.

If you knew that your child had to step onto the battlefield and that you could not be there to fight alongside him, what would you do? Would you just accept this, kiss him goodbye, and hope for the best? Would you trust your child's life to a government employee overburdened with the task of getting hundreds of children he does not know ready for battle? Would you fall down on your knees and pray to God to intervene to protect your child?

No, God helps those who help themselves. You would not send your child into battle with a dull-edged blade, a one-size-fits-all handle, and a few hours of training from a unionized government employee who refuses to be tested on his own fighting abilities and pushes theories in "conflict resolution." You would send your child into the fight with a double-edged fighting knife, custom-fitted for your child's grip, and hours and hours of drill.

It follows that you would not send your child into the economy with whatever educational "theory" happens to be in vogue at the time he is passing through the school system.

If we want America to remain the great country she has always been, more Americans need to realize this basic truth.

4

THE ENVIRONMENT

WHEN I WAS A KID, "ENVIRONMENT" was a word one ran into at a spelling bee. Now we hear it everywhere. And somehow its meaning has changed over the years.

Here is the simple, accurate definition of "environment" in the dictionary I used as a child: "*1*. The act of environing; state of being environed. *2*. That which environs or surrounds; surrounding conditions, influences, or forces, by which living forms are influenced in their growth and development." The dictionary gave an example of the word's usage: "'It is no friendly environment, this of thine' (Carlyle)."

Now look at what one finds under "environment" in a modern dictionary: "*1*. The circumstances or conditions that surround; surroundings. *2*. The totality of circumstances surrounding an organism or group of organisms, especially: *a*. The combination of external physical conditions that affect and influence the growth, development, and survival of organisms." All well and good. But here comes the propaganda:

61

"'We shall never understand the natural environment until we see it as a living organism' (Paul Brooks)."

Well now, three-quarters of the surface of the earth is water, H_2O. Is water alive? It contains living things, yes, but does water itself live? How about sand, rock, lava, soil, the gases in our atmosphere? Of course they are not living. Mr. Brooks's statement is idiotic, but it could be useful as a definition—of the word "agenda."

There is more. The modern definition continues, "*b*. The complex of social and cultural conditions affecting the nature of an individual or community." That is utterly false. The ethereal and (in developed nations) ephemeral social and cultural conditions are not part of the environment. The words "social" and "cultural" may be used as modifiers, as in "social environment" or "cultural environment," but that is all.

Why the falsity? Why the propaganda?

THEY SPREAD LIES—AND AMERICANS BELIEVE THEM

So much has changed since I was kid. For one thing, "environmentalism" has become a religion for some people. It is, in effect, pantheism, and for its practitioners it engenders fanatical devotion and nonsensical beliefs akin to extremist Islam, with its seventy-two virgins awaiting the suicidal jihadist. Thus we have the nitwits who live for years in a tree that does not belong to them to prevent its being harvested (including the woman who fell to her death while moving around over one hundred feet above ground) or freezing their butts off while holding signs that read, "Drilling is killing." Never mind that drilling is no such thing. Truth has little appeal to these people.

Many of the radical environmentalists are mere wackos, but some are very dangerous. When they drive steel spikes into trees scheduled to be harvested, they are endangering the lives of unsuspecting lumberjacks earning an honest living. The arsonists who torch skiing facilities obviously are willing to accept human fatalities for their "great cause."

Lest the reader believe that I am "against the environment" or care nothing for it, I shall be so immodest as to mention that in 1968 I received the Golden Fish Award from the New York State Conservation Council. I was proud of it then and I am proud of it now. The council did and does good work in the general interest. Among other things, it preserves clearings in forests for growth and food for deer, and clears streams to aid fish.

Organizations such as the New York State Conservation Council are not the problem. No, the problem groups are those that attempt to frighten the American public with horror stories of nonexistent threats—all in order to drum up donations. We see this all the time.

Witness, for example, all the groups which spread the lie that we are running out of natural resources—oil, for instance—and that we'll have to give up our fast, powerful, comfortable, and safe automobiles, pickup trucks, and sport utility vehicles and start driving tiny, unsafe, short-range, slow electric cars. *Nonsense*. We have enormous reserves of energy. Disregard for a moment the fact that the world is swimming in oil (much of it untouched, such as the *billions* of barrels in just a tiny portion of the Arctic National Wildlife Refuge), and look at the other resources available just in the United States. By using a process invented by the Germans in World War II, we could easily convert our coal reserves into petroleum, and we have enough coal in the ground to satisfy our energy needs *for the next five hundred years.* We have 2,000 *trillion* cubic feet of natural gas reserves. Our outer continental shelf alone has at least 268 trillion cubic feet of natural gas—and at least 46 billion barrels of oil. And that is just what we know of now. Who knows how much more remains to be discovered?

So why do shortages develop? Breathtaking stupidity coupled with astonishing gullibility. American citizens, made gullible by a public education system that teaches them what to think instead of how to think, and fed a constant diet of liberal propaganda telling them that we are running out of natural resources and that therefore it is immoral to consume energy, are unable to put two and two together and make four.

Take, for example, the California energy crisis that began in late 2000, billed by the politicians as the result of "greedy public utility corporations." That is, of course, a false, stupid, and gratuitous assertion, but most of the gullible California public believed it when just a little independent thought would have exposed the politicians' lie for what it was. Over the past three decades, as the United States added 75 million people to its population, California grew disproportionately. People flocked there to take advantage of the climate and the jobs created by, for example, the new information technology industry—itself a great consumer of energy (as pointed out in the September 2001 issue of the *American Enterprise* magazine, sending a two-megabyte e-mail consumes a pound of coal or eight ounces of oil). The state also welcomed for political reasons the locust swarm of illegal aliens who came by the hundreds of thousands, draining the California taxpayers for the cost of their welfare, their social services (the aliens produced less than they consumed), and the education of their children. All of these people of course increased the demand for electrical power in California. So what was the state's response to this demand? The grand total of new generating stations the state commissioned since 1980 was...zero, zip, zilch. Let's see, huge increase in demand, plus no new supply—what consequence does that suggest to you? If you answer "massive shortage," you have not been listening to the governor of California—remember, it's the greedy public utilities, stupid.

Then we have the solution of the California state legislature. These people ought to wear the popular T-shirt bearing the legend "Hung like Einstein, brains of a horse." Their solution? Not new plants, but a bizarre system that allowed the utility companies to pay market prices for the power they would have to import to meet the huge demand, but then prohibited them from charging their customers more than a regulated rate, which the regulators fixed *below* market price. In other words, buy high, sell below cost—just like the retailer who knew he was losing money on every sale but was confident he would make it up on the volume. Smart. That'll fix the greedy bastards! It sure did. They went bankrupt.

So when this result—which anyone with a real brain could have predicted—came to pass, what was the legislature's new solution? Federal price controls. Fortunately, the president of the United States at the time was a man who had been governor of a state that had been smart enough to add twenty-five new generating plants while California was adding none— George W. Bush. President Bush explained patiently to California governor Gray Davis what even someone of the intellect of Alec Baldwin should be able to understand: artificially holding down prices always *increases* demand and *decreases* supply, making things much worse.

Just as dangerous are those environmentalists who wish to control others. Most of these are politicians. They use the same scare tactics. Their goal is not money, however, but new laws and regulations to limit liberties even further. This is a problem not just here in America. Certain zealots want to control all people, no matter their citizenship. As evidence, I give you the Brussels bureaucrats who brought us the Kyoto Protocol on "global warming."

Granted, there is such a thing as global warming. There also is global *cooling,* something the Henny Pennys of the environmental activist world were frantically warning against just a few years ago. The fact is that the earth warms and cools in great, eons-long, periodic swings having mostly to do with the activity of the sun. Good luck trying to interfere with that.

What *is* going on with the temperature of the globe? No one really knows. We have only a minuscule 140 years of surface temperature records, and much of those are suspect because the readings were taken around cities, which are heat sinks. If, however, we give those readings credence, we see that we are on a steady but *slight* warming trend. Newer technology allows far more accurate readings, using satellites to measure the temperature. Though we have only twenty-three years' worth of those readings, they still show that despite the hysteria over global warming, 2001 was an *average* year in terms of temperature.

Ultimately, one can see that (1) there is no cause for alarm over global warming and (2) puny, hubris-filled humans can do nothing about it. The environmentalist wackos are like the man who urinated into the river at bedtime and then blamed himself for the flood the next day. Here is the fact that puts it all in perspective: *The world has been much warmer than it is now for about 95 percent of the past 100 million years,* and we are all still here, doing fine. In fact, if we are warming, the effect has been to quintuple the yields of U.S. crops and double our life expectancy. So much for all the worries about warming.

When, as it inevitably shall, the earth starts to cool again, what will the advice of the environmental activists be? Go out and burn everything available, including the furniture, to generate "greenhouse gases" to save us from the cold? Maybe then we could all go back to burning our leaves in the autumn the way we did when I was a kid and this was a free country.

Those who would control you by inducing you to give up your liberty to avoid chimerical environmental disasters try, among other tactics, to make you feel guilty about consuming energy. Why would you do something so foolish? We have already seen that we have an abundant supply of natural energy resources and that more and more are being discovered daily. In fact, one of the environmentalists' key programs to get us to save energy—recycling—actually *wastes* energy.

When I was a kid, during the Great Depression, nothing was wasted. No one could afford to waste anything. Once a week, a man pulled his horse-drawn wagon along our street to collect rags. How could the ragman make a living this way? Because the rags could be used again; he was providing a service, meeting a demand. This was how recycling worked; it was a marvelously efficient, free-market system. It was called the "junk business." Today, however, the government forces millions of people in hundreds of thousands of communities to waste their time and energy recycling certain goods for no reason.

One of my good friends is in the junk business today. He is a rich man, because, like the ragman, he provides a valuable service. He will buy, at the right price, all the scrap aluminum he can. Why? Because he knows that to refine aluminum from ore takes a huge amount of energy, and therefore it makes good economic sense to recycle aluminum. Rusted iron? Sure. A controlled amount of iron oxide goes into the making of all new steel; he can move it right away. But glass? Are you kidding? Glass is made out of sand. We are not about to run out of sand. Plastic? You know how many different kinds there are? Who is going to waste his time sorting it?

The government, that's who. Thanks to ill-considered, government-mandated recycling, millions of American taxpayers are funding inefficient and wasteful recycling programs. Now the law forces the average citizen, who has plenty to do with his time, to engage in the amateur junk business. What the radical environmentalists refuse to recognize is that, as my friend's business demonstrates, the market is an efficient recycling program that costs the taxpayer nothing. Indeed, the business *pays* taxes.

THE ENVIRONMENTALISTS REJECT PROGRESS

Those who would have you feel guilty about consuming energy must first dose you with a magic drug that will cause you to forget *why* we consume energy. It is as if they want us to ignore all the technological advances that have eliminated so much of the backbreaking work that used to be required of us.

Not especially long ago, our day-to-day existence was one of toil. I remember it from being a kid in the Great Depression. We kept the milk in the *icebox,* not some fancy *refrigerator* that made its own individual ice cubes. We didn't know what "frozen foods" were. The only thing keeping the icebox cool was, you guessed it, ice. Several times a week, a strong man would pull his horse-drawn wagon in front of our house, brush the straw off a heavy block of ice, put a burlap bag on his shoulder, and hoist the block onto his shoulder; then, using great tongs, he would trudge the ice up a flight of stairs to our kitchen area and deposit it into our great, wooden icebox lined with galvanized iron. The ice would keep milk from going sour for a while and butter from melting, but it kept nothing frozen. The icebox consumed no energy, unless you count all the energy the iceman and his horse had to expend.

Nor did we have automatic machines to wash and dry our clothes. Monday was washday. For the typical household, particularly because the Depression often forced three generations to live together in the same home, the laundry took all day. All married women with live husbands were "stay-at-home moms," of course, because they did not have to go to work to pay taxes; there was little work for them in the Depression anyway, and there was little divorce (who could afford it?). The women knew that the laundry was one of their duties. In rural areas, they would have made their own soap out of fat and lye produced from wood ash, but we city dwellers had the luxury of great bars of commercial yellow laundry soap. The women hated it, because it often took the skin off their hands. Arrayed against the basement wall were stone washtubs, each with hot and cold running water. A special gas-fired heater produced the hot water. Today the government would classify it as an explosive device: You turned on the gas—you had to let it run a little, *but not too much*—then stood back and poked at it with a long, lighted wooden "kitchen" match. *Swhishhfaa*WHOOP! it would go, and all was well. (If it went BANG!—well, I wouldn't be alive to tell about it!) The wash went into the end tub first, to soak. Then the women transferred it to the other tubs and rubbed it, first with the yellow laundry soap, then on the washboards— wooden boards with corrugated metal fronts. Then the laundry went into the rinse tub, and so on. Finally, the wash was consigned to the dryer. It was called the sun. If it was raining, then the women hung the laundry on clotheslines in the basement.

Then there were the heating and air-conditioning systems. Today we are accustomed to having our homes at comfortable temperatures all the time, no matter the outside conditions; in fact, now we can magically adjust thermostats to have different settings for separate areas of the house. Yet when I was a kid, the only air-conditioning we knew was in the movie theater, which advertised it on a great banner that read, "AIR COOLED!" People didn't care what the movie was in July or August—they went for the cool. If we wanted to keep the temperature down in our home, we had to lower heavy canvas awnings to keep the sun out. All the windows were opened all the way, and on each floor a small General Electric oscillating fan moaned away endlessly, moving the stagnant hot air around and affording psychological comfort only. The fans consumed energy, but not much. The lights didn't use much energy either, because we kept them off unless they were absolutely necessary.

Heating did consume energy, literally tons of it, in the form of Blue brand anthracite (hard) coal. During the heating season, a big chain-drive Mack truck would regularly park at the curb in front of our house and a stream of men would haul huge canvas sacks of coal from the truck up to our coal bin, the opening to which was about ten feet from the doors to our hot-air furnace. Every morning and every night, my father and I would affix a big iron crank to the grate fitting and rack it back and forth to shake the ashes down into the ash pit, and then, shovelful by shovelful, "bank" the fire with fresh coal. After closing the fire-pit door, we would adjust the damper to ensure slow burning, then open the ash-pit door and shovel out the ash. When the ash can was full, we would have to carry it down the stairs to the street for collection. All this work spread fly ash and coal dust everywhere, much to the dismay of the women, who saw all their good work at housecleaning threatened twice a day. Fortunately, the effort was worth it, because the heating system worked. The heat came up into the house through great round piping that led to "registers," or openings in the floor; then again, rooms could be quite chilly except for the area around the registers.

As for transportation, we did not have an automobile until 1940. We did not need one in the city and could not have afforded one anyway. Most weekends, we visited my father's sister in the exurbs. First, we—my father, my mother, my little sister, and I—walked two blocks to the bus stop. The bus took us to the railroad station in about twenty minutes. The train took us to the suburb in about an hour. From there, we took the trolley car to the exurb; that was about another hour. Then we walked across the railroad tracks and about a mile to my aunt's house, uphill all the way. Very energy-efficient, very healthy— and very long and tiring, especially for my mother.

When we moved to the exurb in 1940, we finally got a car. We needed one: the nearest bus or trolley stop was a mile away at least. My father bought a 1938 Packard Super Eight. It had pistons like buckets, massive wheels, wall-climbing torque, and a big three-speed stick shift in the middle of the front floor. The steel of the body was so thick that if a strong man had put on a boxing glove and punched the car with all his might, he would have broken every bone in his hand—and would not have even dented the steel. The car probably got about twelve miles to the gallon of premium at eighteen cents per gallon, but it was worth it. It was a *Packard.* They had stopped making the only better car produced in the United States (and maybe the world), the Duesenberg. Those cars were *big,* they were *heavy,* and most of all, they were *safe.*

When my father had to travel to the West Coast as fast as possible, he took off at dawn in the finest airliner of the day, a DC-3. It cruised west at about 200 miles per hour and landed at dusk. Then my father and the other passengers would have to transfer to a steam-engined passenger train that let them off at dawn at an airfield, where they boarded another DC-3 to continue the flight west. These days, I have flown commercially, aboard the Concorde, at 1,346 miles per hour (that's twice the speed of a .45-caliber bullet leaving the muzzle of a Colt 1911A1 military pistol), and traveled from New York to London in exactly three hours and eleven minutes. Of course, the Concorde consumes massive amounts of fuel, but when you have to get there yesterday, it's worth it.

So all these technological advances consume energy. Is that all? What is the problem? Environmentalists seem to reject the idea of progress. Do they want to go back to the days of hauling ice into the icebox, spending entire days scrubbing laundry, maintaining coal-fired furnaces twice a day, and taking days instead of hours traveling a few thousand miles? Do you want that, or do you enjoy having refrigerators, washing machines, advanced air-conditioning and heating systems, and modern airliners, not to mention wide-screen digital televisions, laptop computers, and cellular telephones?

The truth is, there is nothing to feel *guilty* about when it comes to energy consumption. Since 1970, we have made our electrically operated devices 30 to 50 percent more efficient. We have also vastly improved the quality of our lives by consuming 60 percent more power since 1980. Why not? The power is available. Even had we not the great reserves of natural resources we have discussed, there remains the fact that France today generates 75 percent of its electricity from *nuclear* plants.

Uh-oh, I've said that dreaded word. How awful. The citizens of the United States have become so frightened of the word "nuclear" by listening to fools that the medical community has actually eliminated the word from the name of the most important of our lifesaving devices developed in recent years. Now I'm really going to scare you: the real name of the famous magnetic resonance imaging device, the MRI, is *nuclear* magnetic resonance imaging device. "Oh, my God, doc! My sister was in one of those last year! How much time does she have left?" Hey, no one even caught a cold at Three Mile Island. Get a grip.

Indeed, "Get a grip" should be your refrain when some radical environmentalist tries to get you to stop "wasting energy." These wackos have it backwards. We the people aren't the enemy; the federal government is the enemy.

Look at what has happened with automobiles. The federal government, through its Corporate Average Fuel Economy (CAFE) standards, has forced the auto industry to reduce the size and weight of the automobiles we drive. According to a

National Highway Traffic Safety Administration study, from 1975 through 1985 our automobiles shrank ten inches in wheelbase and became one thousand pounds lighter. A *USA Today* report states that because of the smaller, less safe cars mandated by the government, more than 47,000 Americans have already lost their lives.

Americans, not being stupid, reacted. They have abandoned their unsafe, government-mandated motorized roller skates and are now traveling in big, heavy pickup trucks and sport utility vehicles (the infamous SUVs). I drive 140 miles per day, round-trip, and I have to get there—my listeners in Florida and Arizona do not want to hear that I am not on the air because of a snowstorm in a part of the country I did not have the good sense to leave. So I commute in a three-quarter-ton-capacity Chevrolet Silverado HD (for heavy-duty) four-wheel-drive, off-road-equipped, extended-cab pickup truck, powered by a 300-horsepower, overhead-valve, turbo-supercharged diesel engine with 520 pounds-feet of torque—an engine the government had nothing to do with. It gets nineteen miles per gallon at sustained speeds of seventy-five to eighty miles per hour (the average of all vehicles on I-95) and is so powerful that it requires an Allison five-speed big truck automatic transmission. It has lights all over it so everyone can see me coming and get out of the way. It is all black and the license plates say "XFBI." If someone in a little government-mandated car hits me, it is all over—for him. Even my passenger is safe from having his head taken off by one of those government-required killer air bags. I have a switch to turn it off.

When I want to ride for sheer pleasure, I have two Harley Davidsons to choose from, and neither one has been fooled with by the government. Finally, when I *really* want to put the hammer down, I drive my 1991 Lotus-designed, LT-5-engined ZR-1 Corvette with double overhead cam, four valves per cylinder, and two fuel injectors per cylinder—which John Lingenfelter modified to turn out 520 horsepower and 469 pounds-feet of torque at the rear wheels from six liters of displacement. It is good for zero to sixty in under four seconds, can top two hundred miles per hour, and is torch red. The license plate reads "H2OGATE"—not that you'll be able to read it when it flashes by, its wake turbulence blowing the Greenie Weenies' enviro-buggies into the weeds where they'll feel more at home.

YOUR LIBERTY AT STAKE

One of this country's founding principles is that a man's private property should be secure. Perhaps the most sinister aspect of the so-called environmental movement is that the enviro-radicals want to have control over what you do to or with your private property. To them, your liberty is not an issue. This has to stop.

When I was a kid, if my father wanted, say, to build a garage on his property, he would build it—it was his property. If he wanted to cut down a tree for any reason, or no reason, he would cut it down—it was his tree. If the government wanted some of his land for a public purpose, it had to pay him fair market value or it could not have the land.

It's not so simple anymore. Mrs. Liddy owns three acres of waterfront property on the Potomac River, just south of Washington, D.C. Not long ago, our neighbor, an architect, wanted to build something on his own land. The government said no, you may not. It had arbitrarily assumed authority over all the land within a thousand feet of the shoreline along every tributary of Chesapeake Bay and along the entire bay itself. The Potomac River empties into the Chesapeake many miles from where our neighbor's property lies. Government agents also assumed authority over our friend's land because they claimed that a small patch of it (about six by ten feet, as I recall) was a "wetland." The land was dry as a drunk's throat in the morning, but never mind. It seems that the Army Corps of Engineers has said, in effect, that every "wetland" is a "navigable waterway" and, therefore, under the government's authority. About the only thing you could navigate on the patch of land in question was a lawnmower, but my neighbor had to finance a costly lawsuit to beat the greedy enviro-bastards.

Mrs. Liddy also encountered the government's ridiculous incursions on private property. One of the trees in front of Mrs. Liddy's waterfront house died. She was afraid not to cut it down because if it fell, it might hit someone in her driveway, who might sue. Yet she was afraid that if she did cut it down, the government would sue her. (Unlike her husband, Mrs. Liddy does not like lawsuits. I, on the other hand, have three going on at the same time as this is written and will go to trial with the devil himself. As my attorney has said, "The word 'settle' is not in Gordon's vocabulary.") I told Mrs. Liddy she was sued if she did and sued if she didn't, but she thought of a way out. She had the state of Maryland send out a forester, who took one look at the tree and *(surprise!)* said, "Yeah, it's sure dead." We cut it down without incident.

When I was a kid, it would have been absurd even to contemplate what the government reaction might be to your cutting a tree down on your own property. But this is what the radical environmentalists have wrought. When you think about it, is it not ridiculous that my wife could not *immediately* remove a potential threat to human beings because she was worried what government bureaucrats might say about the value of a dead tree?

So remember what to tell the radical environmentalists if you care about your liberty: *Get a grip.* You don't need bureaucrats in Washington telling you what to do with your own land. You don't need to feel guilty about taking advantage of technological advances that save you from backbreaking labor. You don't need the federal government, scared by the environmentalists' shrieking about "global warming" and "disappearing" natural resources, to make you drive an unsafe car just so you can get a few more miles to the gallon.

If you don't want the environmental radicals to seize any more of your liberties, stand up for your rights. You have sense enough to drive a big truck or SUV. Climb into it, drive to your congressman's open house, and tell him to get with the program. While you're at it, get yourself some bumper stickers saying:

MY OTHER VEHICLE IS AN AIRCRAFT CARRIER

INVITE RALPH NADER OVER FOR SPOTTED OWL STEW

NO MORE MILLIONS TO MOVE A HOSPITAL TO SAVE A
WORTHLESS INSECT

As for me, I'm firing up my Duramax Diesel to join you,
and slapping on a bumper sticker of my own that says:

WHEN I WAS A KID, THIS WAS A FREE COUNTRY—
LET'S GET IT BACK THAT WAY!

5

THE MILITARY

ON 11 SEPTEMBER 2001, I had a strong sense of déjà vu. That morning, sitting at my desk in the Washington, D.C., studio from which I broadcast my radio program, I was studying the five newspapers I read daily to prepare for the broadcast. When I looked up at the television monitor, I saw smoke billowing from one of the towers of the World Trade Center. The newscaster reported that an airliner had hit the tower, and suggested idiotically that the plane had been misdirected by air traffic control— as if an airline captain would follow faulty instructions and fly into a building! Then I saw the second plane smash into the other tower, and suddenly I was an eleven-year-old again, sitting on the Oriental rug on the floor of my family's living room. There, on 7 December 1941, I listened to the radio report of the Japanese air raid on Pearl Harbor, and another idiot saying that "the Japanese are an excitable people and this does not necessarily mean war." I knew it meant war then, and I knew it meant war now.

On 11 September, the United States was rudely reawakened to the reality of war. After terrorists struck at our homeland, claiming more than three thousand civilian lives, we began fighting a global war against terrorism—what our president, George W. Bush, has called "a new kind of war." But new or not, war is always with us. As Plato observed more than two thousand years ago, "Only the dead have seen the end of war."

Yet, time and again, we have failed to heed Plato's warning. On 1 September 1939, when war broke out in Europe, America's armed forces were smaller than those of the Netherlands and Portugal, our navy smaller than that of Romania—all because we had foolishly considered World War I, "The Great War," to be "the war to end all wars" and had disarmed. Then, just a few years after our victory in World War II, when the United States was fighting Communists on the Korean peninsula, our government was forced to pay enormous sums for surplus military equipment that it had sold as scrap in 1946 and 1947. After that war, we disarmed again—as we did after the Vietnam War and the Cold War. We never learn.

Some might take comfort in the knowledge that America was incredibly unprepared for World War II and still won. But back then we were saved from the consequences of our folly by our fortunate geography—three thousand miles of ocean off one coast, six thousand off the other. Our homeland was safe from attack; not even a long-range bomber could reach the continental United States. Much has changed since 1939, however; today, a city-destroying missile can reach us from the other side of the world in half an hour.

Moreover, recall how the entire nation mobilized for World War II. I remember it clearly. By war's end, the United States had more than *16 million* men under arms, this at a time when the nation's population was only about 140 million. To get some sense of what this was like, consider that, to be proportionate to the way things were in 1945, our current military would have to have some *33 million* men on active duty. Today, however, we have only about 1.4 million serving in our active-duty armed forces. Only after the heinous terrorist attacks on American soil and the beginning of our global war on terror have our armed services begun to hit their recruiting goals.

Because of the mass mobilization in World War II (almost 12 percent of the population was active-duty military), almost every family in the land had at least one member who either was in the armed forces or had been recently. As a result, when I was a kid, Americans knew what the military was all about—the commitment our servicemen had to make, their dedication, their courage. Our president understood the military culture. Our congressmen understood it. The doctors and lawyers understood it, as did the plumbers, electricians, truck drivers, farmers, auto-workers, painters, carpenters, teachers, policemen, firemen, and all the others. They all understood it because, in the argot of today, they had "been there, done that, got the T-shirt." Except for "T-shirt," substitute "medals for battle wounds and valor."

Today, however, when active-duty military personnel make up less than one-half of 1 percent of the nation's population, Americans are largely ignorant of what the military is all about. So we have allowed our armed services to suffer mightily in the past decade. As we will see, mistakes were made during what was hailed as a great victory over Saddam Hussein's Iraq in the

Gulf War. But the problems began in earnest when a plurality of American voters foolishly voted in the physical and moral coward Bill Clinton as commander in chief of the armed forces.

Thanks to the damage that was subsequently wrought, the United States is forced to prosecute its global war on terror with a military that is in far worse shape than it should ever be. During President Clinton's tenure, the U.S. Army was reduced from eighteen fighting divisions to a mere ten, two of which were not combat-ready. The Navy went from 583 ships down to 371; the Air Force went from 366 bombers to 208. Now we are in another long, protracted war, one estimated to last ten years and to require military action to effect "regime change" in perhaps half a dozen Middle Eastern nations. We were able to defeat a highly unpopular government in Afghanistan with Special Forces and the Air Force assisting indigenous rebels. But to conquer Iraq, an estimated 200,000 troops will be needed. We delay because, as of this writing, we are not prepared.

Let us hope we fix the damage quickly. Some of it, tragically, is irreversible.

WHY A MILITARY IS NECESSARY

Before discussing the various problems that have developed in the American military in recent years, one must answer a fundamental question: What is the *purpose* of our armed forces?

When I was a kid, no one would have even thought of asking such a basic question. Everyone knew the answer. The ridiculous changes that have been forced on our armed forces, however, make it clear that Americans have lost sight of what the military is supposed to do.

The military has but one *raison d'être:* to project power by locating, engaging, and killing the enemy, destroying all the assets that enable him to resist further, and then occupying and holding his territory. War is a dirty, ferocious, and bloody business; as General William Tecumseh Sherman memorably put it, "War is hell." It calls upon men to perform beyond all reasonable expectations of physical and emotional stamina and bravery, even unto death. Veterans of extended combat become remorseless killing machines who are sustained by their allegiance to one another and to their unit. Their mission takes precedence over everything, including their lives.

If the military's sole purpose is to project power, it follows that we want our armed forces to be as strong as possible. The world is a very dangerous place, and if our military is not prepared to the utmost, others can take advantage of our weakness. With a strong military, the United States can say confidently, "Yea, though I walk through the Valley of the Shadow of Death, I shall fear no evil. For I am the most dangerous son of a bitch who ever set foot in this valley!" This is not to say that the United States should be a bully nation that forces other countries to do as we demand or suffer the wrath of our military might. We should, however, advertise throughout the world, *by our deeds,* that we are fully capable of defending our interests against any threat, anywhere, anytime. Power is deterrence.

To understand how military power ought to be used, consider the difference between Julius Caesar and Jimmy Carter.

Though they were confronted by similar challenges, their responses were completely different—and the responses go a long way toward explaining why Caesar is forever remembered as a great leader and why voters removed Carter from office after one failed term.

In November 1979, Jimmy Carter received word that the American embassy in Teheran had been sacked and our diplomats taken hostage. Similarly, one morning Caesar was informed that a tribe in the Gallic territories had accosted his Roman emissaries and killed them. Both leaders understood that if they wished to be able to conduct foreign relations in the future, they had to ensure that the world respected their diplomatic corps.

Nevertheless, Carter seemed to be paralyzed; he did not know what to do. The Iranians were blindfolding our emissaries and parading them before angry mobs on the streets of Teheran, humiliating all Americans in the process. The president's response? Send Iran's diplomats home, freeze Iranian assets held in the United States, and restrict trade with the Islamic fundamentalists who had recently captured control of what remained of the once dominant Persian Empire. Then he waited—for more than a year. When he finally authorized a rescue mission, it was a fiasco: several of the aircraft crashed into each other and burned in the middle of the Iranian desert. After he aborted the rescue mission, Carter reverted to his preferred tactic—waiting. As a result of President Carter's failure to defend his emissaries, American diplomats suffered a rash of bombings and other assorted acts of terror.

Julius Caesar, on the other hand, immediately sent his legions into Gaul to battle those who had laid hands on his emissaries. After defeating the enemy, Caesar's troops methodically slaughtered all the males remaining alive and sold all of the women and children into slavery. From that time forward, Caesar's diplomats served unmolested.

Again, power is deterrence. Julius Caesar understood that; Jimmy Carter, forever chasing an elusive Nobel Peace Prize, knows nothing about the exercise of power.

THE PROBLEMS BEGIN

When I was a kid, American leaders understood what it meant to project power. In recent decades, though, the United States has too often failed to fulfill its commitment to the American people.

When we as a nation decide that a threat in the world is so vital to our national interests that we are willing to ask some among us to risk their lives to protect our country, it is our moral obligation to achieve the mission we set out for ourselves, and to do everything possible to ensure the safety of those we put in harm's way. Strangely, some of our most pressing problems emerged during what many consider to be a brilliant exercise of American military might—the Gulf War. After Saddam Hussein's Iraq invaded Kuwait, President George H. W. Bush vowed to Saddam and the world that "this aggression will not stand." In late February 1991, after a mere one hundred hours of ground combat, U.S. forces made good on that vow, driving Iraqi forces out of Kuwait.

Unfortunately, President Bush then ignored the advice of one of the greatest generals in the history of warfare, Napoleon: "When you set out to take Vienna, take Vienna." General Norman Schwarzkopf, the commander of our troops in the Gulf, was prepared to destroy the fleeing Iraqi troops, but others, including General Colin Powell, the chairman of the Joint Chiefs of Staff (and now secretary of state), counseled Bush to end the fighting. They said, in effect, stop short of Vienna.

President Bush listened to the Powell contingent and ended the Gulf War prematurely. Why?

First, Bush had achieved his United Nations mandate to remove Iraqi troops from Kuwait.

Second, at the time the Iraqi forces were expelled from Kuwait, a mere three hundred Americans had been killed, whereas battlefield projections anticipated that more than ten thousand would be killed in an assault on Baghdad.

Third, our own intelligence officers and our allies warned that some significant force should be left in Iraq to avoid a complete power vacuum, which would guarantee instability in the middle of the world's largest petroleum reserves and bring dramatic price increases in the world's oil market.

Fourth, Iraq's forces, though not destroyed, were weakened to the point where they were no longer capable of projecting power in the region or threatening their neighbors.

Finally, General Powell suggested that Americans would look cruel if we destroyed "defenseless" Iraqi troops, who were retreating with no air cover.

Apparently, nobody counseled President Bush that allowing Saddam Hussein to remain in power, and permitting him to keep a significant army on which to rebuild, would send a very dangerous message to the world (including such potential menaces as Iran, North Korea, China, and Serbia): America does not have sufficient will to make her enemies pay the ultimate price for stepping onto the battlefield with Uncle Sam.

Americans celebrated our great victory in the Gulf War, but most failed to appreciate the dangerous precedents that had been set. President Bush was quite right about the United Nations mandate, which was only to "expel" Saddam Hussein from Kuwait, not to remove him from power. When I was a kid, however, American leaders worked for the *American people,* not global interests or global governments. As commander in chief, Bush was responsible for the long-term benefit of the *United States,* not the United Nations.

Something is wrong when the president of the United States asks the United Nations for permission to use *American* forces to defend *American* interests *before* he seeks the authority of the American people's representatives in Congress.

Bush's decision to end the Gulf War prematurely betrayed another worrisome development: American leaders have deluded themselves that war can somehow be sanitized. When I was a kid, our leaders knew, with Sherman, that war is hell. War is locating, closing with, and destroying the enemy by fire and maneuver. It is justified killing. It is ugly and dirty. There really is no getting around that. We should not send our sons to war unless our vital security interests are at stake. But when we do, we had better embrace the horror and be better at it than our enemies.

During the Gulf War, the Bush administration sold the American public on the fantasy that war does not have to be hell, that it can be sterile. The Pentagon held daily news conferences during which it showed videotapes of "smart bombs" that hit their targets from afar with little likelihood of "collateral damage," a euphemism for dead civilians not targeted. In fact, the vast majority of ordnance dropped during the Gulf War was old-fashioned iron gravity bombs, not the high-tech stuff that made the nightly news. But the lesson was that, somehow, war had changed; it really did not have to be hell.

This is dangerous. By convincing themselves that war did not have to be hell, American leaders came to act as if war *must not be* hell. This translated to the failure to pursue proper objectives. In Iraq, desperate to avoid incurring American casualties and, at the same time, looking "cruel" in their prosecution of the war, Bush, Powell, and the others practiced kinder, gentler warfare— which really meant they had weak stomachs. Is this the legacy of Grant, Patton, and Eisenhower? Remember, in order to achieve critical military objectives at D-Day, General Eisenhower had been prepared to accept 75 percent casualties among airborne troops. During the Second World War, the United States lost *1.08 million* men. That is just about the number of people we have serving in our entire armed forces today.

So what was the upshot of the foolish decision not to take Vienna? Saddam stayed in power and had an army to support him. He took America's failure to push on to Baghdad as a sign of weakness, and he felt bold enough to make an attempt on the life of George H. W. Bush when the former president made a trip to Kuwait shortly after leaving office. By that point, Bill Clinton was our commander in chief, charged with the task of standing up to Saddam Hussein. Of course, he gave Saddam nothing but a slap on the wrist.

Needless to say, things only got worse.

THE COWARD AS COMMANDER IN CHIEF

Twice in 1969, once in the spring and again in the summer, the Arkansas draft board called on a young man named Bill Clinton to don his country's uniform in wartime. Mr. Clinton, however, wanted some other young man to fulfill his draft board's quota, so he manipulated the system, using such highly placed friends as Senator J. William Fulbright to help him dodge the draft. Twenty-three years later, when Clinton was running for president, his evasion of the draft became news. Over and over again, however, we were told by the media that prior military service was not a requirement for a commander in chief, and ultimately 43 percent of the American electorate decided the character flaws that caused Bill Clinton to send someone else in his place were not serious enough to warrant keeping him out of the White House. The American people placed him in command of our armed forces even when it was known that he had not only actively worked to avoid serving in uniform but had also written that he empathized with his friends who "loathed the military."

When I was a kid, such a man could not have been elected municipal sewer inspector.

Clinton was not commander in chief long when we learned what the price for electing him would be, who would pay it, and why.

After ordering American troops in Somalia into harm's way by changing their mission from feeding the hungry to hunting down and arresting warlords, the Clinton administration committed the cardinal sin of putting political considerations above the safety of U.S. troops. Secretary of Defense Les Aspin flatly turned down the on-the-scene military commander's request for equipment to protect his troops. Since the new mission required quick-reaction forces, the commander in Somalia had wanted M1A1 Abrams tanks, the only vehicle in the American inventory that could withstand Somali anti-armor rounds. Why was the request turned down? The answer would not emerge for several months, but it turned out that Aspin had denied the request because it would appear "too offensive."

That wretched act, subordinating the safety of American military personnel to personal political concerns, cost the lives of eighteen American fighting men sent in to rescue the crew of an American aircraft shot down by the enemy. Because the rescuers had been denied the equipment they needed, heavily outnumbered U.S. Rangers had to shoot it out with a Somali warlord's militia until *Malaysian* armor, under *UN* command, could get to the scene. Criminal!

Then came this stunner from the commander in chief when Delta Force briefed the president about the tragic loss of life in

Somalia: As the briefer related the bitter fighting to retrieve the dead, President Clinton interrupted him to ask, "Why didn't they just leave [their dead behind]?"

The shocked silence was finally broken when Clinton was told, "Sir, we don't *do* that."

The man who had fled his country rather than serve it in uniform in time of war demonstrated yet again not only his personal unworthiness to command our military, but also his total lack of understanding of the brave men under his command. The bond that fighting men share is based upon an elementary bargain: I'll die so that you and the rest of our unit can advance one hundred meters, and all I ask is that you bring back what's left of me to my mom or wife so she can bury me with our family in our hometown.

Only someone profoundly ignorant of history and culture would not understand that. We are still trying to recover our dead from Vietnam. In the Korean War, General "Chesty" Puller loaded his wounded Marines into trucks and chained the frozen corpses of the dead on the outside to bring them back to their families. Perhaps, having wasted his time at Oxford, Bill Clinton was not familiar with Homer's *Iliad*. In ancient Greece there was no greater humiliation for a soldier than to be left unburied, his body eaten by vultures and dogs. Homer tells how Achilles defiled the body of Hector by fastening his corpse to a chariot and dragging it three times around the city of Troy. Sound familiar? Does that bring to mind a certain photograph, featured prominently in America's newspapers, of Somalis dragging a dead American soldier through the streets of Mogadishu? Obviously that photograph meant nothing to President Clinton. Why else would he ask so stupid a question of men whose combat boots he was not worthy to lace? When I was a kid, this country had real military and political commanders. A real commander would have put the world on notice that treating the corpses of American soldiers with disrespect carries with it a severe penalty—he would have carpet-bombed Mogadishu, the scene of the crime. In World War II we incinerated Dresden with no such provocation.

What was Bill Clinton's response? He sent a U.S. Air Force jet to pick up the warlord responsible for desecrating the soldier's body and bring him to "peace talks"—which of course led to nothing.

Then again, nothing about President Bill Clinton's dealings with the military should have surprised us. This man not only did everything in his power to avoid military duty, he *loathed* the military. Thus we saw a commander in chief who had no problem sending soldiers into harm's way for personal political reasons, for "photo-op foreign policy"; who diverted military training funds for environmental nonsense and other pet liberal programs for which he could not get the funding he wanted; whose underling used Marine One for a golf trip; who was so arrogant and so ignorant of military decorum that he actually ordered more than a dozen military officers assigned to the White House to pick up trays of hors d'oeuvres to serve Democratic Party contributors (which prompted the furious White House military social attaché to exclaim, "We are military officers, not waiters!").

WEAKNESS SPURS ON THE ENEMY

Under Bill Clinton, America's enemies got away with all sorts of mischief. Time and again the Clinton administration illustrated how weakness breeds contempt and aggression.

North Korea built nuclear weapons, telling the world the program was merely for generating electricity—while refusing to allow international inspectors to view the facilities. President Clinton responded by offering North Korea more than a billion dollars in "energy assistance," but still the North Koreans would not allow inspections.

Closer to home, Cuban jets shot down American civilian aircraft in international airspace. The pilots were part of a group that took to the skies over Cuba peacefully to drop pro-democracy leaflets over Cuban neighborhoods. President Clinton did nothing.

Then there was Iran. Under Clinton, Russia aided Iran's nuclear development, and both China and India helped Iran develop chemical, biological, and nuclear weapons, and their means of delivery, making Iran a threat far beyond the Persian Gulf region.

Then, too, the Communist Chinese government, in its quest for superpower status, stole much of America's advanced military technology. National security investigations revealed that the Chinese Communists had agents of influence in Clinton's Commerce Department, secreting out classified trade documents, and that Clinton had facilitated the export of ballistic missile and satellite technology to China over the vehement objections of the Pentagon. A select bipartisan House committee also revealed that the Chinese had stolen "modern thermonuclear weapons designs" from the United States. It suddenly became clear how: Beijing funneled hundreds of thousands of dollars (at least) in illegal political contributions to the 1996 Clinton-Gore reelection campaign. In short, by pouring money into the Democratic Party's coffers, Red China, an emerging (and hostile) world power, was able to take the leader of the Free World out of the game and acquire sophisticated military technology. We have yet to learn just how deadly President Clinton's actions will be to America's security.

But more than anyone else, it was Saddam Hussein who capitalized on American weakness and Bill Clinton's inability to act decisively. With his usual truculence, Saddam refused to allow United Nations weapons inspectors to do their job in Iraq. Clinton first threatened him with words, then tried to intimidate him by deploying a large U.S. strike force, at considerable expense to U.S. taxpayers. It did not work. Worst of all, Clinton kowtowed to the United Nations. It was the same sort of globalist nonsense we saw with President George H. W. Bush during the Gulf War.

In March 1998, the secretary general of the United Nations, Kofi Annan, announced triumphantly that he had reached "a deal" with Hussein that permitted UN weapons inspectors back in Iraq. Saddam, of course, was simply buying time for himself, since any deal he signed with the United Nations would put U.S. military action on hold. Still, Annan was confident, assuring the United Nations (in a speech broadcast worldwide) that he could "do business with" Saddam. He added that if Iraq were not to comply, "diplomacy may not be given a second [read, twentieth] chance," and he warned Iraq of "the severest consequences" if it failed to honor the terms of the "agreement."

In other words, the United Nations secretary general was using U.S. forces to back up his threat. The U.S. government went along with the deal because it seemed to defang Saddam. But then Annan revealed that if Hussein reneged on the agreement, the United States would still have to get permission from the UN Security Council before it launched attacks on Iraq. Though he objected at first, President Clinton ultimately told Annan that it would be "unthinkable" for the United States not to consult with the United Nations before ordering an attack on Iraq if Saddam violated the new deal.

Why would the U.S. president abdicate his authority to the United Nations? When I was a kid, a confident commander in chief of the world's only superpower, with a massive military strike force in the Persian Gulf, would have told the UN secretary general that he does not speak for the United States when our security interests and American lives are on the line. Further, he would have added that if Saddam violated UN sanctions, we would strike without warning—and without UN approval—every site in Iraq that U.S. intelligence indicated might house chemical or biological weapons.

Predictably, Clinton's globalist approach did not work. In a short time all weapons inspectors were out of Iraq. Key members of the inspection teams were openly critical of the White House. There was growing contempt for the United States within the

ranks of the United Nations diplomatic corps, which was push-
ing for a standing UN army. The American president was in the
midst of a humiliating sex scandal, Saddam was laughing, and
somewhere a man named Osama bin Laden was taking notes.

PERPETUATING THE FANTASY
OF THE "SAFE" WAR

In the Gulf War, President Bush bought into the myth that war
need not be deadly, and as a result we refused to engage the
enemy to achieve our proper objectives. There is another danger in this fantasy of nondangerous warfare: American leaders
convince themselves that if we do not accept casualties, we can
engage in war more often. Under the Clinton administration,
the United States forgot the true purpose of the military.

Look at what happened in Kosovo. Were America's vital
security interests really at stake? The religious and cultural war
in central Europe was horrible and difficult to ignore in this day
of satellites and video, which bring human suffering into America's living rooms. Nevertheless, this conflict was a European
problem that had continued for several centuries, save for the
recent period of totalitarian control enforced by the late iron-
fisted Yugoslavian president, Marshal Tito. President Clinton
could not stop the slaughter in the Balkans with any less a commitment than Tito's—thirty years of occupation by ground
troops. That is not sound American policy. But Clinton did not
think that the old rules applied to him. His political polls told
him that the video and anecdotes of rape, killing, and "ethnic

cleansing" meant that he had to do something. He had the added incentive of trying to build himself a legacy other than the one he and "that woman, Ms. Lewinsky," had so crudely fashioned.

President Clinton saw a chance to persuade historians that Kosovo was the last great struggle of the twentieth century, pitting the forces of globalism against tribalism. If only he could do it without a war. He and his advisors, shockingly devoid of military experience, deluded themselves into believing America could become engaged in the European religious conflict with a new type of military intervention, short of war. Ever the globalist, Clinton conducted the campaign in close cooperation with the North Atlantic Treaty Organization (NATO).

In the spring of 1999, General Wesley Clark, the NATO military commander, said that we would "systematically and progressively attack, disrupt, degrade, devastate and ultimately... destroy the military forces of Slobodan Milosevic." That is the appropriate objective of a military commander who understands the true parameters of war, but it was not what President Clinton and the NATO bureaucrats had in mind.

The effective use of military force requires an integrated and mutually dependent use of air, mechanized, and infantry forces. But Clinton and NATO thought they could follow the Gulf War model of conducting air strikes so that our soldiers would not be at risk. The trouble with this approach was that whereas the Middle East offered the perfect terrain and climate for conducting a precise air campaign with guided munitions—wide-open desert with little or no cloud cover—Kosovo's steep terrain, cloudy skies, and thick forests meant that an air campaign would be effective only if infantry was deployed to support the strikes. Clinton refused to send in ground troops, however, and American pilots had to remain above fifteen thousand feet in order to avoid the anti-aircraft elements that could hide so effectively in the rugged terrain.

This was ridiculous. Have you ever seen newsreel film from the gun cameras of P-47 Thunderbolt fighters attacking enemy railroad trains, tanks, and artillery during World War II? They are behind enemy lines, without ground support, on the deck, flying below the Luftwaffe flak towers. In the Pacific, a P-40 Warhawk fighter strafed a Japanese vessel so low that an enemy seaman's cap became lodged in the plane's air intake. Safe? No. Effective? *Yes!* In Yugoslavia, our pilots were trying to engage the enemy on the ground from *three miles high*.

President Clinton did not care. He did not want to send in ground troops, did not want to sustain casualties. Besides, he had already surrendered his constitutional authority to NATO, which forbade our using ground troops. This came out in testimony before the Senate Armed Forces Committee, when the chairman of the Joint Chiefs of Staff, General Henry Shelton, revealed that the United States could not use ground troops because there was a lack of "consensus" among the nineteen NATO countries. When Senator John McCain of Arizona pressed him on this subject, General Shelton admitted that NATO would not permit the Pentagon to plan a ground war because the Russians did not want it. So there you have it—our draft-dodging commander in chief gave command over the Pentagon to the Kremlin!

By openly stating that he would not engage in all-out war in Yugoslavia, President Clinton gave Slobodan Milosevic the green light to pour in armor and start house-by-house "ethnic cleansing." Clinton, in fact, emphasized the weakness of our position by bombing the very bridges across the Danube that our armored divisions would need to do the only thing that would assure victory in the Balkans: roll into Serbia, and on into Belgrade, to accept unconditional surrender.

The initial reports out of Yugoslavia spun the tale of a huge military victory without a single American casualty. The Clinton Pentagon at first reported that the nearly forty thousand American sorties kept above fifteen thousand feet had "severely crippled" the Serbian military forces. General Shelton told the Pentagon press pool that our air attacks had destroyed more than 50 percent of Serbian artillery and a full one-third of the tanks and armored personnel carriers.

But the truth came out when Serbian tanks, artillery pieces, and troops left their hiding places in the forests to execute an orderly retreat from Kosovo back into Serbia proper. It turned out that many of the targets engaged from high altitude had been crude wooden decoys; American pilots flying three miles above the ground could not have known this. Million-dollar munitions had been wasted repeatedly. The Pentagon's claims were wildly overstated; for instance, only twelve Serbian tanks were confirmed destroyed—a mere *10 percent* of what was originally claimed. Worse, thanks to Clinton's refusal to allow American pilots to fly below fifteen thousand feet, several refugee convoys had been mistakenly attacked because the pilots could not identify the Albanian women and children.

The situation in Kosovo was but one example of how the United States continually misused its military. When I was a kid, everyone knew why we had the Army, Navy, and Marine Corps (the Air Force, then the Army Air Corps, did not become a separate fighting force until 1947): to fight for our country, period. The end of the Cold War, however, saw us embark on far too many "peacekeeping," "nation-building," and "humanitarian" deployments in places such as Haiti and Somalia. These were not the missions for which the brave members of our armed forces were trained. In fact, because of these burdensome, unnecessary, non-war-fighting deployments, essential war-fighting skills deteriorated. (In Bosnia, for example, our soldiers were taught to keep the barrels of their tanks and their rifles down, and to make as much noise as possible when they moved, so as not to frighten civilians—the direct *opposite* of what they are trained to do in combat.) *Warriors must train continuously, or their war-fighting skills atrophy.* Needless to say, 11 September 2001 was a stark reminder that our nation's armed services must always be at the peak of their war-fighting skills.

THE DAMAGE DONE

Now that we are engaged in a worldwide war against terrorism, Americans should be particularly alarmed at the severe decline of our armed forces. In recent years, defense spending plunged to less than 3 percent of our gross domestic product (GDP), the lowest level since America's pre–World War II isolationist period. Meanwhile, the federal government gobbled up our tax dollars; federal revenue was nearly 21 percent of GDP—our highest rate of taxation since we were fighting for our lives in World War II! The lack of proper funding since the end of the Cold War (after which the defense budget was cut dramatically), combined with unnecessary and burdensome peacekeeping and humanitarian deployments, has led to a severe decline in our military preparedness.

In the late 1990s, two U.S. Army divisions were declared unfit for combat. In 1998, the aircraft carrier USS *Enterprise* deployed to the Adriatic undermanned by eight hundred sailors. Half of the Army's divisions have reported too few majors, captains, and sergeants to fill the required billets. *Those are the battlefield leaders of the troops who actually fight our wars.* We cannot just go out and hire replacements. It takes years of training and experience to create them. Until recently, every branch of the armed forces except the Marine Corps was failing at its recruitment goals. (President Clinton's secretary of the Army wanted to resolve the problem by lowering the standards for recruitment.) We were losing pilots and other trained warriors faster than we could recruit and train new ones. And morale was at an all-time low for our volunteer military. It is, of course, little wonder, given how shabbily our military has been treated in recent years. As recently as the year 2000, some twelve thousand enlisted personnel were on food stamps. That is *shameful.* The Clinton administration's solution was not to pay military personnel more for their skilled, brave service to our country but rather to "retabulate" the compensation for the lowest-ranking troops. "Retabulate" meant to "pencil-whip" the statistics so the poor souls were *no longer eligible for food stamps.* Who cares about how they feed their children? Just declare them ineligible and solve the embarrassing political problem of soldiers on food stamps.

And, please, do not be fooled by the recent successful campaign in Afghanistan. The fact is, we are nearly out of select air-delivered munitions, and our ground troop commitment is limited to a few Special Operations and Marine personnel. We could not execute a Desert Storm today. Aircraft lie dormant at Langley Air Force Base in Virginia for lack of replacement jet engines. Marines practice calling fire missions on telephones, because they have no batteries for the radios they must take into combat.

We are now just at the beginning of a protracted global war that will demand the most of our armed services; does all of this not seem alarming?

Also troubling is the decline of American intelligence capabilities. A nation's spies are its eyes and ears. Military intelligence has played a vital role in protecting peoples for thousands of years (the first recorded use of spies is in the Bible—Book of Numbers, Chapter 13, when Israel sent spies into the land of the enemy to learn whether they lived in tents or within walled fortifications and to report on their agriculture). Without verifiable and timely intelligence, a nation treads blindly through the threatening wilderness.

Unfortunately, many liberal politicians fail to understand the critical role that intelligence plays in protecting our society, just as they fail to understand the vital role our military plays. It began in the 1970s, when a few Democrats from the party's emerging left wing were caught up in the dangerous illusion that war was always the result of misunderstandings. These naive idealists believed that countries only built armies because they felt threatened and that the world would really be a nice place if everyone just stopped preparing for war. So these liberals advocated unilateral disarmament, and they grew to detest Americans serving in the military. They also despised our intelligence services, viewing them as conspirators dedicated to fooling the American people into spending millions of tax dollars so that shareholders of defense industry companies could become rich. In due course, in 1973, a special House of Representatives committee chaired by Congressman Lucien Nedzi was charged with the task of investigating the Central Intelligence Agency (CIA) and the Federal Bureau of Investigation (FBI). In fact, I became the only person in United States history to be indicted and convicted of two counts of contempt of Congress when I refused to participate in this attempted destruction of the FBI and CIA. I would not testify when subpoenaed. Others did. Years later, when I was traveling in the rear of an official limousine with then–director of Central Intelligence William Colby, he told me that if he had not testified (he was accused of giving away "the family jewels"), the agency would have been destroyed. He told me that he had saved it, but he understood and appreciated what I had done—or, rather, *not* done.

Though the Cold War has ended, naive liberals still cling to the idea that the intelligence services are harming this nation. In the 1990s they used the CIA's failure to detect Soviet spy Aldrich Ames as an opening to claim that the entire intelligence system needed to be taken down—the exact same claim they were making two decades earlier, long before they knew of Ames's treason.

Not surprisingly, when Bill Clinton became president, he appointed some of the holdovers from the "blame America first" crowd to key positions in the CIA. Thus we had as director of Central Intelligence John M. Deutch, a Clinton appointee who told us that the president's military cuts had not degraded readiness—just a few months before two Army divisions were declared unfit for combat because Clinton's budgets did not provide them with enough fuel and ammunition to train. Deutch also vowed to "cure" sexism by making all the career intelligence officers report to a former Capitol Hill aide who had no intelligence-gathering experience but had the much-needed asset of being female. Even the *Washington Post* labeled the authority that Deutch had given the inexperienced Nora Slatkin "extraordinary."

Thereafter we suffered the redirection of our spy satellites to gather data on alleged global warming and deforestation, rather than on foreign powers that sought to exploit any slips by the world's only superpower.

The current director of Central Intelligence, George Tenet, a Clinton holdover, has been a disaster. His passion has been not intelligence gathering and analysis but rather "diversity" within the agency—a major reason the CIA did not have a clue about the deadly intentions of Osama bin Laden's al Qaeda organization toward the World Trade Center and the Pentagon.

Merely establishing a new bureaucracy called the Homeland Security Department is not the answer. The answer is to force cooperation and coordination among the existing agencies by firing recalcitrant agency chiefs and their deputies and hiring new ones determined and able to change FBI and CIA cultures from dog-in-the-manger to wolf-pack mentality.

SOCIAL EXPERIMENTATION IN THE MILITARY

Americans should be aghast at the social engineering that has occurred in our armed forces, because it has dramatically threatened our war-fighting capability. The military is not supposed to be a microcosm of greater America. It is not a jobs program, or a place for social experimentation, or a venue for political correctness. It has its own culture that has proven, generation after generation, to be effective in supporting its mission—and that mission is to visit death and destruction upon the enemy. Remember, the military has but one purpose: to wage war. It is an organization of warriors, trained and bonded together to such an extent that they will, if necessary, give their lives for the mission and one another.

Why, then, have politicians insisted on foisting on our armed forces pet programs that threaten our ability to wage war?

To begin, women have absolutely no place in combat. Their physical weakness relative to men makes them dangerously unable to perform to male standards. Their sexual difference makes them a distraction and a disruptive force; they interfere with male bonding and unit cohesion even more than the presence of a known homosexual. And such bonding is absolutely essential to the mission, which, of course, is to advance through hell to kill the enemy.

Here is but one example of the bonding technique used to make America's most elite fighting force—one in which there has never been a woman, and in which there never will be, because no woman ever born could meet its demands of physical strength and stamina—the Navy SEALs. The Pacific Ocean is not warmed by the Gulf Stream, as is the Atlantic. To the contrary, it is chilled by the cold-water California Current. One night during training, the candidates are brought at sundown to a Pacific beach and stripped naked. There is a physician in attendance and an ambulance standing by. The water temperature is noted. The men are seated in the surf with their backs to the cold waves that wash over them, chilling them to the bone. When the physician determines that further exposure could be fatal, they are ordered out of the water and seated on the sand in a circle around a small fire. The fire is so small that although they can see it, it provides them no warmth. The only warmth they get is from the press of the naked bodies of their comrades seated to either side of them—hence, more bonding. When it is determined that the men are no longer in danger of death from hypothermia, they are sent back into the cold waves and the cycle is repeated. I know of one night in which the cycle was repeated twenty-two times before dawn, when the sun's warming rays ended the test. For a test it is, to see who will quit under such extreme conditions; in fact, those conditions are *better* than those they may be required to endure in the performance of their duties as SEALs.

The infamous Kelly Flinn case demonstrated just how dangerous the presence of women in the armed forces can be. Lieutenant Flinn was America's only female B-52 pilot, and as a graduate of the U.S. Air Force Academy, she was taught the importance and effectiveness of good order and discipline, high morale, respect, and loyalty up and down a clear chain of command. She knew the military consequences of fraternization and adultery, yet she decided to have sexual relations with an enlisted airman, and later conducted an affair with the civilian husband of an enlisted woman. When the Air Force discovered the second affair and ordered her to stop seeing the airwoman's husband, Lieutenant Flinn disobeyed the direct order; when Air Force investigators questioned her about her harmful sexual behavior, she chose to lie under oath. A court-martial was the appropriate vehicle to relieve Lieutenant Flinn of her responsibilities as a bomber pilot with a nuclear payload.

Consensual sex, even adulterous consensual sex, is not the only problem. It should come as no surprise that some men and women will use their positions of authority (in the military and in the civilian workforce) to pressure their subordinates to engage in sexual acts. (No one needs to be reminded that a governor of Arkansas used the power of his office in an attempt to intimidate a state employee to "Kiss it! Kiss it!") There have been numerous reports of male officers flagrantly abusing their positions of authority by demanding or requesting sex from young women serving below them in the chain of command. In its first week of operation, the U.S. Army's sexual harassment hotline received more than four hundred calls, among them numerous complaints from young females that their *female* superiors had pressured them for *homosexual* sex.

If you wonder how much women affect morale in the military, ask yourself these questions: How does a sailor's wife feel as her young husband deploys for six months aboard an aircraft carrier that she knows will return with dozens of pregnant female sailors and aboard which some female crew are engaging in prostitution? How does her husband feel when he sees assignments made based on sexual favors? To ask those questions is to answer them.

The harsh truth is that when a crew is composed of both men and women (mainly very young men and women, about nineteen or twenty years old, on average), there is a lot of sex between shipmates. That is a fact. No amount of regulation will change that fact. When, as a result of feminist pressure, the USS *Eisenhower* included hundreds of women as part of a crew of several thousand men, the results were disastrous, if not predictable: Thirty-eight of the women got pregnant, fourteen of whom were known to have conceived at sea. Many had abortions. Many were either married themselves or having sex with married male crew members. At least one male crew member videotaped the sexual acts he had with a female shipmate and showed the video to small gatherings aboard the ship. One of the female sailors, of a number who prostituted themselves at sea, made so much money she hired Marine guards to protect her as she took her money to the bank in Naples, Italy. Good order and discipline clearly suffered. Imagine the effect on morale when there is even the suspicion that assignments may be determined by who is having sexual relations with whom among the crew.

The point is this: It's tough enough to land a multiton, twin-engined fighter jet on the short deck of an aircraft carrier in rough seas at night without hundreds of young, hormonal sailors unable to focus on their dangerous duties. Do we really need to do this? Was there something deficient in the job every other ship or aircraft carrier did during fifty years of tours at sea, including some of the most ferocious wars we have ever fought, to warrant so radical a step? I think not.

Another reason for keeping women out of combat is cultural. We send our men to kill and die to protect women and children. In essence, that is what we fight for—our families, property, and freedom. Sending our mothers, sisters, daughters, and wives would defeat the purpose of fighting at all. Of course, it could be dangerous for a member of our armed forces actually to voice this opinion. In the late 1990s, some female fighter pilots asked Captain Dennis Gillespie, the U.S. Navy air wing commander on the carrier USS *Lincoln,* his opinion on placing women in combat aircraft; he said, "I love my wife and my daughter.... [Having them in combat aviation is] difficult to see ... because I have always had this feeling that in this country, the philosophy was that we wouldn't put our women in harm's way." *Burn the heretic!* Gillespie was subjected to a major Navy investigation, which ultimately found him to be deficient in the "communications skills" required to "lead a diverse [coed] Navy into combat." The *Washington Post* reported that Gillespie was part of a broader problem in the military: the prevalence of older warriors who had been educated in all-male military academies and developed as officers in all-male combat units—too much "male bonding," in other words. It seems not to have occurred to this liberal newspaper that such bonding has been responsible for forming the world's greatest fighting force.

All this is not to say that there is no role for women to play in our nation's wars. During World War II, we had the Women's Army Auxiliary Corps (WAAC) and similar organizations for the Navy (WAVES) and the Army Air Corps (WAFS). To avoid all the difficulties we have today, the women were billeted separately, had their own (female) commissioned and noncommissioned officers, and had nothing at all to do with combat. Their motto was "Free a man to fight!" They did a great job, it was a great system, and it wasn't broke—so, years later, they fixed it. Integrating women into the armed forces ruined morale and lowered the standards of just about every service but the U.S. Marine Corps (which does not train male and female recruits together) and Special Operations (which does not accept women).

Political correctness reaches absurd levels when we are ensuring "equal opportunity" for women in the military even when such opportunity does not fulfill the armed services' fighting objectives. For example, with no shortage of American men willing and able to learn to fly high-performance fighter jets, and with no need for more fighter pilots, President Clinton's politically correct Pentagon decided that fighter-jet billets should be open to women—though women were still, quite properly, not permitted to fly in combat. Such training, the politically correct said, was "crucial to an Air Force or Navy career"—in other words, they wanted career opportunities to be "fair." But as anyone with military experience can tell you, there is an awful lot about military life in general, and combat in particular, that is not fair.

Feminists and the politically correct do not want to hear that. When Raytheon Aircraft won a fierce competition to build a new high-performance training aircraft for Air Force, Navy, and Marine fixed-wing pilots, liberal politicians protested, forcing a months-long delay in awarding the contract. Why? They didn't think the Raytheon design was fair to women, worrying that very small, lightweight women could not eject safely from the aircraft. Never mind that the Pentagon affirmed, and the General Accounting Office ultimately verified, that the aircraft easily met congressional demands that the aircraft accommodate 80 percent of the female population—including women as short as five feet tall and as light as 104 pounds. No, the feminists and liberals wanted to spend several *billion* dollars redesigning the aircraft to ensure that it was "user-friendly" for *all* women. Why not redesign for the blind, too? Oh, excuse me, for the "visually impaired," in idiot speak. Many thousands of men have been turned down for flight training because of physical characteristics not compatible with the safe operation of military equipment. They would not let me be a fighter pilot in the Korean War because I wore glasses. Men with flat feet cannot safely operate a pair of combat boots during a fifty-mile forced march. So what?

The damage wrought to our military by providing women so-called equal opportunity has been bad enough, but it is not the only problem. President Clinton's most famous social experiment with our men and women in uniform occurred just after he entered the White House. Obeying the demands of the strong homosexual lobby that had played a key role in his election victory, Clinton attempted to overturn the military ban on open homosexuality. Much to the surprise of the radicals in the Clinton White House, but not to anyone else, all hell broke lose. The U.S. military believes rightly that homosexuality is not compatible with military service, but of course Clinton and his advisors did not understand the military or what it takes to make a strong fighting force. In the end, Clinton could not win out over the Pentagon, which had legitimate reasons for banning homosexuals from the military. The Pentagon cited the threat to military unit cohesion arising from sexual tension, concerns about the effects of fraternization, and the risk of AIDS (homosexuals are many times more likely to have contracted HIV than are heterosexuals, and, in the event of casualties, all soldiers in a unit are part of the same blood bank). Fortunately, in this case military preparedness won out over "fairness." Frankly, however, any policy that encourages dishonesty and pandering—such as "Don't ask, don't tell"—has no place in public policy, either.

Another politically correct development that has hit our armed forces has been affirmative action. The proud United States Marine Corps substituted racial quotas for standards of intelligence, moral and physical courage, and leadership ability in recruiting officers. These are qualities heretofore considered highly indicative of the ability to lead others in battle. What has skin color to do with the capacity to accomplish a mission and keep Marines alive? We have also seen tax dollars going to encourage "diversity" in the military. It has been hard enough for military recruiters just to find enough bodies to replace the droves exiting the ranks. Only the swell of patriotism following 11 September 2001, combined with a sluggish economy, has enabled the military to meet its recruiting goals.

THE AMERICAN WAY

When I was a kid and this was a free country, we were forced into a world war for which we were ill prepared. Then, as now, military morale was low, because Congress, in order to save money in the midst of the Depression, had cut the already woefully inadequate pay of the armed services. Then, as now, military equipment was in short supply. New recruits were being taught the manual of arms with broomsticks because there were not enough rifles to go around. Then, as now, we were challenged by "Axis" powers.

Today, organized terror, spawned by radical Islam, seeks to attack our assets at home and abroad and kill our civilians, including women and children. Nazi and Imperial Japanese fanaticism is matched by the jihadists of Islam. Even more threateningly, Communist China challenges us, not only on its side of the Pacific Rim but also on ours. Its tentacles already enclose both ends of the Panama Canal. It lusts after our faithful ally Taiwan no less than did Hitler the Sudetenland and Hirohito the Philippines. It boasts our own warhead designs atop its ICBMs, which can reach cities on our West Coast.

We have no more time to listen to fulminating feminists, proselytizing poofters, the environmentally ill, devotees of diversity, sycophants of sensitivity, academic acolytes of armament atrophy, multilateralist UN worshipers, and assorted other politically correct castrati. The terrorists are crazy fanatics. There is no other option but to seek them out and kill every last one we can find. We must remember the Zulu leader Shaka's counsel: Never leave an enemy alive on the ground behind you, for he will rise up to strike you again. Regimes that support or aid terrorists in any way must be annihilated. To accomplish this will take at least ten years and armed forces trained to be ferocious, *in*sensitive killers and destroyers. We don't have to go back to Caesar's Roman Legions for our model. In 1945, Eleanor Roosevelt, wife of the late president, wrote an article in what was then the most-read periodical in the United States, the *Saturday Evening Post*. In it she argued that the Seventh Infantry Division, which had successfully assaulted the suicidally fierce and fanatic Imperial Japanese on Okinawa, ought not to be permitted back into the United States until they had been "re-civilized." Why? Because the Seventh Infantry Division of 1945 was exactly what we need to train our present-day soldiers to be. They went into battle with stakes lashed to the sides of their tanks; upon each stake was the impaled head of a Japanese soldier. There are photographs of our soldiers sitting atop a high pile of rotting enemy corpses, eating their midday rations from their mess kits.

As for the Chinese, they are dangerous, but they are not crazy. For them, the Roman dictum will work: *Si vis pacem, para bellum* (If you want peace, prepare for war). We must deal with them as we did with the Soviets: become and stay so powerful, militarily and economically, that they will not dare to attack us or our allies. That requires not only preparedness but also the will to strike when appropriate. We need to act so as to leave no doubt in any corner of this world, no matter how remote, that country singer Toby Keith spoke for all America when he sang:

> This big dog will fight
> When you rattle his cage
> And you'll be sorry that you messed with
> The U.S. of A.
> 'Cause we'll put a boot in your ass
> It's the American way

6

OF MEN AND WOMEN

So God created man in his own image; in the image of God He created him; *male and female* He created them.... And the Lord God said, "It is not good that man should be alone; I will make him a helper *comparable* to him" [emphasis added].
—GENESIS 1:27, 2:18

FOR SOME FIVE THOUSAND YEARS, there was general agreement that the terms "male" and "female" would not have been used in Genesis had there been no distinction between them (God enjoying an excellent vocabulary). While men and women are "comparable" (able to be compared; deserving comparison; similar), they are not "identical" (absolutely alike; same).

So it was when I was a kid and this was a free country (somewhat more recently than the writing of Genesis, although some mornings it feels like it was that long ago). Back then, as had been true throughout history, one was free to hold and state, without fear of contradiction or condemnation, that men and women, while both fully human, differed in matters that went beyond "plumbing." For example, in World War II it never occurred to either men or women that women should be sent into combat against Waffen SS Panzer divisions or the Imperial Japanese Army. Anyone holding that view would have been run out of town. Today, anyone *not* maintaining that view suffers the consequences: students are run off campus, and members of our

119

armed forces, no matter how highly decorated for valor, can have their military careers destroyed.

Somehow, in just a few generations, we have turned our back on a fundamental truth: *Men and women are different.* There is nothing wrong with saying that. So many of this country's problems stem from our refusal to accept reality, to address issues head-on. Political correctness has so warped our lives that many are appalled when someone stands up and states the obvious.

The truth is, it is idiotic to accept the 1960s notion that, plumbing aside, men and women are identical, and that the plumbing business is of no significance. Ten thousand people swearing that a horse is a dog does not make a horse a dog. I have no quarrel with those who advance the proposition that women are superior to men or vice versa. To so hold is to admit that men and women differ. I say, *"Vive la différence!"*

In discussing the differences between men and women and the consequences thereof, I shall be referring to the male and female sexes, not "genders." The word "gender" has to do with grammar. It means the classification by which words are grouped as masculine, feminine, or neuter. The word "sex," on the other hand, means the total characteristics, structural and functional, that distinguish male and female organisms. It also means the attraction between the sexes and sexual intercourse. The word "gender" is *not* a synonym for the word "sex." Even the politically correct nitwits who misuse the word "gender" in that way have not yet, that I can discover, referred to "genderal intercourse."

Please note also that I do not use that abomination "his or her," because I am aware that under the rules of the English language the feminine is subsumed by and included in the masculine. I also want to make clear that what I have to say here are not intended to be universal statements. I am only too aware that people are a varied lot and that even one exception destroys the asserted universality of a characteristic. Nevertheless, certain universal statements about men and women are valid: for example, all are created by God, and each and every one is loved by his Creator.

UNDERSTANDING MEN AND WOMEN

The primary cause of the difficulties men and women experience with each other, the so-called War Between the Sexes, is their inability to understand one another—not as individual persons, but as men and women. This has led to some humor on the Internet. By women:

1. The nice men are ugly.
2. The handsome men are not nice.
3. The handsome and nice men are homosexual.
4. The handsome, nice, and heterosexual men are married.
5. The men who are not so handsome, but are nice, have no money.
6. The men who are not so handsome, but are nice and have money, think we are only after their money.
7. The handsome men without money are after *our* money.

8. The handsome men who are not so nice and somewhat heterosexual don't think we are beautiful enough.

9. The men who think we are beautiful, who are heterosexual, somewhat nice, and have money, are cowards.

10. The men who are somewhat handsome, somewhat nice, have some money, and, thank God, are heterosexual, are shy and NEVER MAKE THE FIRST MOVE!!!

11. The men who never make the first move automatically lose interest in us when we take the initiative.

NOW . . . WHO IN THE HELL UNDERSTANDS MEN?

Then there is this gem, *purportedly* by a woman writing over a century ago:

INSTRUCTION AND ADVICE FOR THE YOUNG BRIDE *on the Conduct and Procedure of the Intimate and Personal Relationships of the Marriage State for the Greater Spiritual Sanctity of This Blessed Sacrament and the Glory of God*

By Ruth Smythers, beloved wife of the Reverend L. D. Smythers, Pastor of the Arcadian Methodist Church of the Eastern Regional Conference

Published in the year of our Lord 1894, Spiritual Guidance Press, New York City

To the sensitive young woman who has had the benefits of proper upbringing, the wedding day is, ironically, both the happiest and most terrifying day of her life. On the positive side, there is the wedding itself, in which the bride is the central attraction in a beautiful and inspiring ceremony, symbolizing her triumph in securing a male to provide for all her needs for the rest of her life. On the negative side, there is the wedding night, during which the bride must pay the piper, so to speak, by facing for the first time the terrible experience of sex.

At this point, dear reader, let me concede one shocking truth. Some young women actually anticipate the wedding night ordeal with curiosity and pleasure! Beware such an attitude! A selfish and sensual husband can easily take advantage of such a bride. One cardinal rule of marriage should never be forgotten: GIVE LITTLE, GIVE SELDOM, AND ABOVE ALL, GIVE GRUDGINGLY. Otherwise what could have been a proper marriage could become an orgy of sexual lust.

On the other hand, the bride's terror need not be extreme. While sex is at best revolting and at worst rather painful, it has to be endured, and has been by women since the beginning of time, and is compensated for by the monogamous home and by the children produced through it. It is useless, in most cases, for the bride to prevail upon the groom to forego the sexual initiation. While the ideal husband would be one who would approach his bride only at her request and only for the purpose of begetting offspring, such nobility and unselfishness cannot be expected from the average man.

Most men, if not denied, would demand sex almost every day. The wise bride will permit a maximum of two brief sexual experiences weekly during the first months of marriage. As time goes by she should make every effort to reduce this frequency. Feigned illness, sleepiness, and headaches are among the wife's best friends in this matter. Arguments, nagging, scolding, and bickering also prove very effective, if used in the late evening about an hour before the husband would normally commence his seduction.

Clever wives are ever on the alert for new and better methods of denying and discouraging the amorous overtures of the husband. A good wife should expect to have reduced sexual contacts to once a week by the end of the first year of marriage and to once a month by the end of the fifth year of marriage.

By their tenth anniversary many wives have managed to complete their child bearing and have achieved the ultimate goal of terminating all sexual contacts with the husband. By this time she can depend upon his love for the children and social pressures to hold the husband in the home. Just as she should be ever alert to keep the quantity of sex as low as possible, the wise bride will pay equal attention to limiting the kind and degree of sexual contacts. Most men are by nature rather perverted, and if given half a chance, would engage in quite a variety of the most revolting practices. These practices include among others performing the normal act in abnormal positions; mouthing the female body; and offering their own vile bodies to be mouthed in turn.

Nudity, talking about sex, reading stories about sex, viewing photographs and drawings depicting or suggesting sex are the obnoxious habits the male is likely to acquire if permitted.

A wise bride will make it the goal never to allow her husband to see her unclothed body, and never allow him to display his unclothed body to her. Sex, when it cannot be prevented, should be practiced only in total darkness. Many women have found it useful to have thick cotton nightgowns for themselves and pajamas for their husbands. These should be donned in separate rooms. They need not be removed during the sex act. Thus, a minimum of flesh is exposed.

Once the bride has donned her gown and turned off all the lights, she should lie quietly upon the bed and await her groom. When he comes groping into the room she should make no sound to guide him in her direction, lest he take this as a sign of encouragement. She should let him grope in the dark. There is always the hope that he will stumble and incur some slight injury which she can use as an excuse to deny him sexual access.

When he finds her, the wife should lie as still as possible. Bodily motion on her part could be interpreted as sexual excitement by the optimistic husband. If he attempts to kiss her on the lips she should turn her head slightly so that the kiss falls harmlessly on her cheek instead. If he attempts to kiss her hand, she should make a fist. If he lifts her gown and attempts to kiss her anyplace else she should quickly pull the gown back in place, spring from the bed, and announce that nature calls her to the toilet. This will generally dampen his desire to kiss in the forbidden territory.

If the husband attempts to seduce her with lascivious talk, the wise wife will suddenly remember some trivial non-sexual question to ask him. Once he answers she should keep the conversation going, no matter how frivolous it may seem at the time. Eventually, the husband will learn that if he insists on having sexual contact, he must get on with it without amorous embellishment. The wise wife will allow him to pull the gown up no farther than the waist, and only permit him to open the front of his pajamas to thus make connection. She should be absolutely silent or babble about her housework while he is huffing and puffing away. Above all, she should lie perfectly still and never under any circumstances grunt or groan while the act is in progress.

As soon as the husband has completed the act, the wise wife will start nagging him about various minor tasks she wishes him to perform on the morrow. Many men obtain a major portion of their sexual satisfaction from the peaceful exhaustion immediately after the act is over. Thus the wife must insure that there is no peace in this period for him to enjoy. Otherwise, he might be encouraged to soon try for more.

One heartening factor for which the wife can be grateful is the fact that the husband's home, school, church, and social environment have been working together all through his life to instill in him a deep sense of guilt in regards to his sexual feelings, so that he comes to the marriage couch apologetically and filled with shame, already half cowed and subdued. The wise wife seizes upon this advantage and relentlessly pursues her goal first to limit, later to annihilate completely her husband's desire for sexual expression.

This one, too, has become popular on the Internet. It paints quite a picture. It also raises the question, Why *do* men and women have so much trouble understanding one another?

To answer that question, I will leave aside the very young and focus on mature adults. Young people's inability to understand the opposite sex has much to do with their woeful and pathetic inexperience. (In fact, those of high school age, or those recently out of high school, of either sex, have no business even contemplating marriage because they will be in so far over their heads they will drown quickly.)

Even for mature adults, the source of the inability to understand the opposite sex is the inability to understand hormones.

When a man, driving along a highway, conducting a pleasant conversation with his wife in the front passenger seat, is suddenly and deliberately cut off by another male and floors the accelerator to hurtle forward in pursuit at ninety miles per hour to cut off the offending driver, his wife will scream at him to *stop!* She wants him to stop behaving like ... *a man!*

The wife is quite correct that her husband's behavior is stupid, dangerous, illegal, and illogical. What she does not appreciate, however, is that, initially, his behavior is not chosen. It is dictated by a testosterone-fueled rage that has triggered a massive flow of adrenaline. The answer to her screamed *"What are you thinking?!"* is that he is not thinking at all. He is in the thrall of a primal emotion, and her screaming is itself extremely dangerous, because it is distracting him at a time when he needs all his driving skills to avoid an accident as he does what he is compelled to do—engage in combat with another male who has challenged his manhood. The driver, like the man he is chasing, is an Upper Paleolith for whom the ten thousand years since the advent of agriculture has been but a fraction of the time necessary to evolve sufficiently to adapt to the world of today.

Of course the wife does not understand her husband; she has in her body but the tiniest smidgen of testosterone, the ultra-powerful hormone that gave her husband his height, muscle mass, masculine features, facial hair, deep voice, aggressive response to challenge, and constant interest in, and readiness for, sexual intercourse. To his wife, her husband is like all other men in that he is an idiot. A woman who is cut off while driving would never react that way. It would not occur to her that the person who cut her off was challenging her femininity. She would just conclude (correctly) that the offender was an imbecile, a bad driver, and, yes, a man.

Does the powerful influence of testosterone and adrenaline deprive a man of his free will and render him not responsible morally for his actions? No. He is, after all, made in the image and likeness of God, and that means two things: (1) his soul is immortal and (2) he has free will. He also has an intellect and a moral responsibility to use it. But just as the law recognizes the difference between a crime committed coolly, after thoughtful contemplation (with malice aforethought), and one committed in a blind rage (a crime of passion), one must understand that testosterone, particularly in combination with adrenaline, diminishes a man's capacity to exercise free will and engage his intellect. Women particularly need to understand this. They have virtually no testosterone in their bodies and are, therefore, ignorant of its powerful effect on men.

Men, on the other hand, need to understand that to a woman the words "wants," "needs," "desires," and "moods" are synonymous. Women are affected by hormones to a far greater extent than are men. Between the onset of puberty and menopause, a woman has a varying amount of estrogen surging through her body, and the level of estrogen contributes to her mood—whether she is happy or sad, interested or anxious, angry, weepy, frustrated, eager, energized, sentimental, patient, or amorous. Absent estrogen, a woman would have no libido, no sexual desire at all. In fact, after menopause—that is, when her childbearing years are over and she has no biological need for sexual intercourse—her estrogen level falls so low that she has practically no desire. Typically, the only way to restore her libido, should she wish to do so, is through synthetic hormone replacement therapy, usually by wearing a transdermal patch.

During her childbearing years, after a woman menstruates, she experiences a great surge of estrogen, triggered by sensors in her brain, that stops her period. For about a week thereafter, until the flow of estrogen levels off, many women will be sexually insatiable and highly orgasmic. Some women even have pet names for that time—"my horn-dog week," for example. Lucky is the man who understands this, and unlucky the man who is under the illusion that women, like men, are sexually "good to go and ready to launch" at all times. Would that it were true, but it is not. Indeed, one of the great secrets of life (a secret to men, anyway) is that many women have sexual intercourse with men because they have to, to get what they want. This is particularly true after marriage.

MARRIAGE AND FAMILY

Marriage is an unnatural, extremely difficult institution that is absolutely necessary for the continuation and advancement of the species. It can be, under rare circumstances, extremely rewarding to the participants. That the divorce rate is so high bespeaks a failure of bachelors and spinsters alike to understand the opposite sex (or, in the case of the young, even themselves).

Marriage is unnatural, because we are all, at base, Upper Paleolithic hunters (males) and gatherers (females). As recently as ten thousand years ago, men hunted game while women gathered nuts and fruit. Following their natural instincts, the strongest males got the most women and impregnated them as often as they could. This was good for the nomadic tribe, for it increased the tribe's size, which was useful in territorial warfare against other tribes. The only education needed was related to hunting, gathering, and the making of crude weapons, clothing, and temporary shelter, along with some useful rudimentary hygiene, geography, and battle tactics.

The institution of marriage arose as agriculture replaced nomadic wandering, for with agriculture and the advent of private property came the need for a family to till the land and harvest crops. Even then, however, as a holdover from the old days, multiple wives and concubines were the rule for those men who could afford them (see the Old Testament). The more complex society that was developing meant that there was much more to teach the young, and this education took a longer time to complete. Thus we see the need for a long-term commitment between men and women, for a stable family that can train its young over a long period of time. The need for marriage and stable families has only grown greater over time: today, in the Information Age, a youth must complete a huge amount of both education and training—he needs knowledge and skills—before he can expect to succeed in our highly competitive society.

As we have seen, however, our instincts have not evolved sufficiently to adapt to the relatively new institution of marriage. For marriages to succeed, men, in particular, must be able to suppress their strongest instincts, and, if the truth be told, some suppression is necessary for some women at certain times of the month. Yet it is easier for women to do so because of the vastly greater investment they have in the stability of the family.

Marriage alone does not make the family; a family is not formed until the couple has a child. At that point, the relationship between the husband and wife changes essentially and irrevocably. When I was a kid, children locked in a marriage. These days the arrival of a child or children sometimes destroys a marriage. That happens because the normal woman goes through the pregnancy (not easy), puts on the weight, and has to manage everything she always did. It dawns on her that a faceless, nameless character has invaded her beautiful body—a character she grows to love more than she does herself.

A woman's life is changed forever by the act of giving birth. It is such a phenomenal emotional event that it overwhelms most women; they don't realize, until the baby is about a year old, what a wonderful thing they have produced. In that first year, the wife is still expected to do it all—everything she did before the baby came, on top of caring for the baby, which is in itself a round-the-clock job requiring that she work herself to exhaustion daily without the restorative of sleep at night. Her husband (and society) expects her to "snap back" into her prepregnancy body in a matter of weeks, but as the saying goes, "It takes nine months to get there and it takes nine months to get back."

During this time, many, if not most, husbands do what they do best: they take all the credit and put forth little effort. Women grow wise very quickly. They grow resentful. They are no longer interested in taking care of their husband, because he has proven to be such a jerk. They now use sex as a tool, a weapon, or bait to get what they want. Women finally realize, "I'm doing it all now. What do I need him for?" They work up the courage to go, and these days half of them do.

When I was a kid and this was a free country, women really liked men. Bad experiences with men could change that, of course, but generally women liked and admired men and looked forward to marriage and family, to staying home to do the hard but joyful work of making a home for their man and their children. That has changed. Why? In large part, it is the men's fault. At the heart of the problem, I suspect, is that men have allowed the government that they control to impose such a massive tax burden on married couples that it is impossible for the average woman to stay at home to care for her family. She must also get a job just to pay the family's tax burden. Mom has to drop off her children at the child-care center before school and pick them up at the end of a long day at work, giving the kids just enough time for homework, supper, and "hello" to Dad before they are off to bed. "What kind of a life," a woman asks herself, "is this?" It's hell, that's what it is, and men created it.

Then there is the feminist fantasy that women can "have it all." Sounds great until you're close to forty and the eggs are so old that any pregnancy is high-risk at best; even if everything works out, you will have the fun of being referred to as your child's grandmother at the PTA meeting. Even though it was women who created that fairy tale, it was politically correct males in politics, academe, and the media who cheered, "Yeah, baby!" and perpetuated the myth until the trap snapped shut, and now there's no escape except for those women fortunate enough to have paired off in matrimony with an exceptionally successful . . . *man!*

MAKING MARRIAGE WORK

In spite of all of the foregoing, if a couple can get over the trauma to their relationship brought about by the advent of children, and can pool fairly their intellectual, educational, financial, and, above all, emotional and spiritual resources, marriage can be deeply rewarding, emotionally *and* physically. Herewith a few tips on how best to achieve such a rewarding union.

Before all else, you must determine *when* to marry. Do not marry until you are a mature adult with some experience of life and of the opposite sex. Marrying before the age of twenty-five is an invitation to disaster. Moreover, marry only when you can honestly say to yourself, "I cannot, and do not want to, live the rest of my life without this person." To be able to say that, you must know the other person *very* well, intellectually, emotionally, and physically. The man who marries an inorgasmic woman has only himself to blame; the woman who does not know her own body has only *her*self to blame.

There are some people, men and women, for whom sex is not a big deal. Let us hope they find each other. For the rest of us, sex is a *huge* deal. The absence of satisfactory sex will kill a marriage quickly. A woman may hold on to it "because of the children," but many women will go outside the marriage to get satisfactory sex. Virtually *all* men in those circumstances will do so. A couple would be well advised to do whatever is necessary—however out of the mainstream (e.g., acting out fantasies)—to preserve the spontaneity and freshness of their sex lives. Remember, too, that sex, however pleasurable, cannot reach its potential without deep, honest, emotional, loving passion.

No marriage should be entered into without total honesty between the prospective mates. It is vital to have the attitude, "I don't care what you did in your past, or with whom. I bless whatever and whoever made you the person you are today, with whom I am so in love."

The Golden Rule works for marriage as well as it does for everything else. If you had a very bad day and you take it out on your spouse, you will get it back.

In addition, always keep in mind that words are very powerful. Let us say that you are having a disagreement and your spouse has said something you find offensive. You know exactly the right comeback to score a devastatingly effective win. *Don't say it!* Words once uttered can never be taken back. They can be forgiven but will never be forgotten (especially by women, who forget *nothing*), and things said in moments of anger will accumulate, festering and eroding the relationship until finally it is gone.

Another firm rule: *Don't complain!* It quickly becomes a bad and damaging habit. If there is a problem, wait until the right moment, then raise it as a matter of discussion to make the relationship more enduring.

Men, there is, in any relationship between men and women, a question you will be asked: "Does this [dress, coat, sweater, whatever] make me look fat?" It is not the answer that will put you in the doghouse; it is *how rapidly* you answer the question. Hesitate for a nanosecond and, whether the answer is yes or no, you will not be believed and will suffer the penalty for all eternity. Practice answering such questions *instantly.*

Women, I have a news flash for you: *Men have egos.* It is normal and understandable to a man for his ideal woman to notice that another man is good-looking or desirable. Your man will require reassurance, however, that "Of course, he's nothing like *my* hot stud!"

What does a man want? He wants a woman who is smart, funny, and passionate; whom he finds beautiful; who is right-up-front, look-you-in-the-eye, honestly and overtly sexual, highly orgasmic, and utterly devoted to him. He knows that the children have to come first, but he wants his woman to go *way* out of her way to make it up to him—to make him feel that he is her ideal man and that she loves him to the utmost of her capacity to feel and express love.

What does a woman want? What all women *really* want is to know deep within their heart that they are loved unconditionally—no matter how they look when they wake up, how they smell, how long or straight their hair is, how skinny or fat they get, or whether their man's lunch is packed with goodies. Women want men to continue to open the car door and stand up when they enter a room. Women want men to speak to them politely, without vulgar references. Women want most of all to know, and, more important, to be *told,* that their devoted love is not being wasted, and is reciprocated.

Amen.

7

SURVIVE OR PREVAIL?

WHENEVER I GIVE A LECTURE, whether I am speaking to college freshmen or great-grandparents, to a group of forty or four thousand, I invariably begin by asking this question: "By a showing of hands, how many of you have heard it said of a third party, intended as a compliment, that he is 'a real survivor'?"

A forest of hands greets me every time.

Yet, as I tell my audiences, to be called a survivor is *not* a compliment. Consult a dictionary. "To survive" means merely "to continue to live or to exist." What kind of way of life is that? But flip back in the dictionary to another verb, "prevail." Look at *that* definition: "to overcome; to gain the victory or superiority; to gain the advantage; to have the upper hand, or the mastery; to win; to triumph; to be victorious." What a completely different way of life!

Most people in the world are survivors. There is nothing dishonorable about being a survivor, but a survivor does not take full advantage of his resources. In other words, surviving is a waste of human potential.

It is not difficult to see the advantages of being a prevailer rather than a survivor. Why continue simply to exist when one can "triumph" in life, "have the upper hand"? I have made a study of those who prevail in life, and fortunately, anyone can become a prevailer. But if you want to prevail, you must know *how* to do it and have the discipline to keep on a course that avoids mere survival.

So who is the prevailer? We all encounter obstacles in life, but the prevailer is someone who, no matter what difficulties present themselves, always comes out on top. You undoubtedly know of someone like this. Take the dentist who is stripped of his license to practice. What does he do? He begins a brand-new career in the great soybean fields of the Midwest—and within six months is known as the "Soybean King."

When I met Frank Smith on my tour of the beaches of Normandy where the D-Day assault occurred, I knew I was in the presence of a prevailer. After our victory in World War II, in which he played no small part, Frank went home and became a master machinist. Even today, he runs his own machine shop and takes only the most difficult jobs. Frank is not merely surviving.

It is no coincidence that a prevailer like Frank Smith is from the generation that fought and won the total war that was World War II—the group of Americans that has rightfully come to be known as the "Greatest Generation." Another of the 16 million men who served in our armed forces during the Second World War was my friend and neighbor Joe Foss, now in his late eighties.

In the Pacific theater, the United States stopped playing defense and went over to offense on 7 August 1942, when Admiral Chester Nimitz landed U.S. Marines on the island of Guadalcanal. The battle, on the island and over it, lasted five ferocious months. Joe Foss arrived at Henderson Field, which the Marines were still fighting daily to hold, in early October as executive officer of VMF 121, touching down with his squadron of Grumman F-4F Wildcat fighters.

Joe is a big bull of a man who dominates a room as soon as he walks through the door. He could address the crowd at Yankee Stadium from the pitcher's mound without a microphone and no one would miss a word; if he whispered, people would strain to hear, because they just naturally want to hear what he has to say. He's a born leader—and a born fighter.

Joe, a poor boy, lost his father as a teenager and was raised on a South Dakota farm that had no electricity. He shot game birds on the wing for food and earned his way through college and flying lessons by working at a gas station. After graduation he enlisted in the Marine Corps, went through Officer Candidate School and Flight School, and, because of his extraordinary skill as a pilot, was assigned as an instructor. When the Japanese attacked Pearl Harbor, however, Joe was no longer happy as a flight instructor. It took him nearly a year to get to Guadalcanal, but once there, he made up for lost time. Because I'm his friend, any description I might give of Joe's deeds over Guadalcanal would be subject to a charge of exaggeration, so I will let the official record speak for itself:

FOSS, JOSEPH JACOB

Rank and organization: Captain, U.S. Marine Corps Reserve, Marine Fighting Squadron 121, 1st Marine Aircraft Wing.

Place and date: Over Guadalcanal, 9 October to 19 November 1942, 15 and 23 January 1943.

Entered Service at: South Dakota.

Born: 17 April 1915, Sioux Falls, S. Dak.

Citation: For outstanding heroism and courage above and beyond the call of duty as executive officer of Marine Fighting Squadron 121, 1st Marine Aircraft Wing, at Guadalcanal. Engaging in almost daily combat with the enemy from 9 October to 19 November 1942, Capt. Foss personally shot down 23 Japanese planes and damaged others so severely that their destruction was extremely probable. In addition, during this period, he successfully led a large number of escort missions, skillfully covering reconnaissance, bombing, and photographic planes as well as surface craft.

On 15 January 1943, he added 3 more enemy planes to his already brilliant successes for a record of aerial combat achievement unsurpassed in this war. Boldly searching out an approaching enemy force on 25 January, Capt. Foss led his 8 F-4F Marine planes and 4 Army P-38's into action and, undaunted by tremendously superior numbers, intercepted and struck with such force that 4 Japanese fighters were shot down and the bombers were turned back without releasing a single bomb. His

remarkable flying skill, inspiring leadership, and indomi-
table fighting spirit were distinctive factors in the defense
of strategic American positions on Guadalcanal.

That citation was for Joe Foss's Congressional Medal of
Honor. Stunningly impressive as it is, it doesn't give you the full
flavor of the man. Unlike many combat veterans, Joe is not reluc-
tant to discuss the war, I suspect for two reasons. First, he is ever
mindful of those who "didn't make it back," who gave their lives
for the freedoms we are guaranteed under our Constitution, and
he never fails to remind the living of what we all owe to those
who gave everything they had, or would ever have, for us. Second, his experience in combat is a national resource that he is
called upon regularly to share with those who are currently serving, or who might in the future be called upon to serve, in the
U.S. military.

Joe also is blessed with a wonderfully self-deprecating sense
of humor. He once remarked to me, "You know, I'm a Japanese
ace, too. I destroyed five American planes." He was referring to
his being shot down in combat as he challenged superior numbers. He told me of one air battle in which his plane was damaged and, as he tried to nurse it back to Henderson Field, a
Japanese Mitsubishi AN-6 Zero stayed right with him all the
way down to the runway, its machine guns blazing. The armor
plate behind Joe's back stopped the slugs that otherwise would
have killed him but, of course, stopped none of the slugs to its
right and left. They tore up his control panel and destroyed his
instruments, forcing him to land "dead stick." He lived, and as

soon as he was on the ground he got out of the wreck and into a fresh plane to go fight more Japanese.

I don't know the details of how Joe Foss was shot down, but he did tell me that the Navy's method of aerial gunnery didn't work. He said that it wasn't until he realized this, and started leading Zeros the way he used to shoot ducks on the wing, that he started to rack up his air-to-air victories. Shows you what a boyhood with a gun can do for a man.

To give you some idea of the ferocity with which the Pacific war was fought, Joe once told me that when he flew against the Japanese, he took along a .22-caliber long-rifle pistol in addition to his service handgun. Why? First, if he had to bail out over enemy-controlled jungle, he hoped the relatively quiet report of the .22 would enable him to shoot food to sustain himself without being discovered by the enemy before he could work his way back to friendly territory. Second, if he *was* detected, he had no intention of being taken alive by the Japanese. He intended to stand up and keep shooting, with both his service pistol and the .22, until he was killed. Joe didn't want to have happen to him what had happened to other captured flyers. The Japanese strung them up alive and cut steaks from their naked buttocks, which they then cooked and ate before the eyes of their mutilated prisoners, who were slowly bleeding to death. (Perhaps now you will understand why, during the battle for Okinawa, the Seventh Infantry Division's tanks went into battle with stakes lashed to them upon which were impaled the heads of dead Japanese soldiers.)

When Joe Foss was awarded the Medal of Honor, to his dismay he was taken out of combat. He spent the rest of the war trying to get back *into* combat—and when the Korean War broke out, he tried *again*. This time he went straight to the top, personally asking the chief of staff of the United States Air Force to allow him to fight again. The answer was, "Not only no, Joe, but *hell* no!" Joe's still pretty mad about that.

He didn't let it slow him down, though. Among his additional services to his country, he founded the South Dakota Air National Guard and became its general, and became governor of that state, commissioner of the American Football League, and president of the National Rifle Association. But when you try to praise Joe Foss, he just shakes his great head and says, "You gotta remember those great guys who didn't have a chance to do anything more because they didn't make it back."

Joe Foss—*there* is a prevailer, a person who overcomes the most difficult obstacles and flourishes.

CLEAR THINKING,
CLEAR COMMUNICATION

One of the most important characteristics of those who prevail is that they are utterly candid and never engage in the sort of fuzzy thinking that plagues so many Americans these days.

Think about the new, politically correct America. We turn away from and deny the harsher aspects of reality through the deliberate *mis*use of language. As evidence I give you the sea of euphemisms in which we swim. The crippled metamorphosed first into the "disabled" and then into the "physically challenged." Used cars are "previously owned vehicles." The deaf are "hearing-impaired." Jungles and swamps have become "rain forests" and "wetlands"—because no one will vote, much less send in their "maximum emergency contribution," to save a mere "jungle" or "swamp." The Bible says that the poor will always be with us, but that is not really true; now we have the "underprivileged" (an oxymoron). I served time in nine different prisons, but not one of them was ever called a prison. Some were "penitentiaries," although I never saw anyone therein who was penitent (*I* certainly was not!). Others were called "correctional institutions"; I was in prisons for years, and I never saw them correct a single soul. Plus, there were never any prisoners; we were referred to as "inmates," as if we were all sent there to lose weight.

Those who prevail never abuse language that way. They know that precision and clarity of language lead to precision and clarity of thought. Prevailers are most candid with themselves, even if it means facing a harsh reality; if one does not acknowledge an obstacle, how can one overcome it? They know that others misuse language to avoid facing reality, which gives them an advantage they can, and do, exploit. Because the prevailer does not make the mistakes so common to others, he is often thought of as cold or emotionless. That is not true. It is just that he understands what makes us tick as human beings.

REASON

Proudly we denominate ourselves as *Homo sapiens,* the rational or thinking animal. Our Creator issues each of us an M1A1 human brain, the situs of reason. Yet, as I saw in the many autopsies I attended as a prosecutor, beneath that brain is another brain, much smaller than the first and with far fewer convolutions. About the size of a fist, it sits atop the spine and is usually referred to as the "old brain," the "midbrain," or the "crocodile brain." (Were you to place it next to the actual brain of a crocodile, you would be hard put to distinguish one from the other.)

That old brain plays a critical function. As you read this, you are not commanding your eyelids to blink to lubricate your eyes—yet it happens. You do not order your heart to beat or your lungs to inhale and then exhale. That old crocodile brain is controlling those and all the other autonomic functions of your body. It has another important function of which you might not be aware. Until now, as I call your attention to it, you were not conscious of the pressure of the floor upon the bottom of your feet. It was always there, but until you read that sentence you didn't notice it. In fact, you and I and everyone else on earth are being bombarded constantly by a huge mass of stimuli, so much so that if it all got through to our conscious minds at once, we couldn't handle it. We would become catatonic. That doesn't happen because we have a protective filter—that ancient organ, the crocodile brain. The old brain is like a secretary that lets through only the most important messages so we are not completely overwhelmed.

So as much as we think of ourselves as rational beings, we are governed to a great extent by the crocodile brain—that is, by instinct. And when it comes to instincts, "modern man" is no different from the Upper Paleolithic hunter-gatherer. We are all equipped with instincts that are never, ever wrong—for the world as it existed some ten thousand years ago.

Therein lies the problem, particularly when instincts are prompted by the real human motivator, emotion. That Upper Paleolithic combination of instinct and emotion can be extremely dangerous in today's world. Consider what happens when a plane stalls. I am a Federal Aviation Administration–licensed pilot, and trust me when I tell you that any fixed-wing aircraft, at any attitude and any airspeed, can undergo a phenomenon called "stall," which has nothing to do with the operation of the engine but rather means that the wing stops flying and you're headed toward the earth with the gliding angle of a brick. If you were the pilot in this situation, what would instinct instruct you to do? Pull back on the controls, of course. Yet what is really motivating you is emotion—in this case, fear, fear for your very life. So instinct is telling you to pull back on the controls, while fear is *screaming* at you: *"Pull up! Pull up, or you're going to die!"*

Unfortunately, that is exactly the *wrong* thing to do. You'll go into an unrecoverable spin and screw yourself into the ground. What you must do is totally *ignore* your instincts *and* emotions and tap into your M1A1 human brain, wherein is located all that you learned in flight school. There you will find the counterintuitive instruction to push the controls *forward,* steepening the dive until the relative airflow over the wing is sufficient to give it lift. Then, and only then, may you safely pull back on the controls and pull out of your fall toward the earth.

So there you have it. Obey your Upper Paleolithic instincts and emotions and you will surely die. Use your intellect and ability to reason, and live.

Yet the vast majority of us, in some of the most serious decisions to be taken in our lives, do not engage our M1A1 brain.

When evaluating a prospective business partner, a mature businessman will conduct due diligence, checking credit ratings and so forth. But when considering the most important partnership into which he will ever enter—marriage—the same man will resort to instinct and emotion. This is not the way to prevail in life. Just ask the airline pilot I know who has been divorced *five* times. When I asked him if he had learned anything from his experience, he sighed and said, "Yes: You marry a pair of legs, you *get* a pair of legs."

Or take the teenage boy who saves all his money to buy a car. Into it he will put the highest-quality fuel and oil, and he will maintain the vehicle scrupulously. But how does he treat the body God gave him, the only body he will ever have? With junk food. Cigarettes. Alcohol. Perhaps even drugs. All the result of the herd instinct and emotion.

Those who prevail don't make such mistakes. They are perfectly capable of feeling emotion when appropriate, but the M1A1 is always engaged and in control. Having gained that self-discipline, what does the prevailer do next? He observes the world around him and tries to learn from it.

PHYSICAL AND MENTAL STRENGTH

On the vast plains of Africa roams the cheetah, an amazing animal that, for a short distance, can outaccelerate my Lingenfelter-modified 520-horsepower ZR-1 Corvette. He kills every few days, not because he is depraved or because he wants to impress females with his machismo, but because he must eat. The cheetah is a pure predator. His prey: the wildebeest, an animal that travels across the veldt in huge herds. Each wildebeest herd is dominated by a great, powerfully muscled stag, a magnificent beast with needle-sharp horns and hooves that can slice through flesh like a razor.

Could the cheetah defeat in mortal combat the great stag that leads the wildebeest herd? Perhaps, but we do not really know. In the history of Africa, the cheetah has not once attacked a lead stag. Never. Why? Because the cheetah is not stupid. Even were he to win that momentous battle, he would be so badly wounded that he would be unable to hunt for a long time and would probably starve, or be vulnerable to other predators. So upon whom does the cheetah prey? A very young wildebeest; a very old wildebeest; a sick wildebeest; perhaps an already wounded wildebeest. What is the constant? Always a *weak* wildebeest.

Now, we know there are predatory people, predatory organizations, and predatory nations in this world. The lesson is the same whether we are talking about cheetahs or humans: the pure predator always avoids the strong and is drawn ineluctably to attack the weak. Those who prevail understand that, and so they make themselves strong, both physically and mentally. The prevailer works hard to ensure that he is never the victim.

As a boy, I was physically small and weak. (My lungs still bear tubercular scars, and to this day I react positively to the tuberculosis patch test.) So I made myself crude barbells by filling an assortment of tin cans and buckets with concrete and connecting them with pipes. For my lungs, I became a runner. By the time I was a senior in prep school, I was a member of a state championship cross-country team. I weighed only 128 pounds but was strong enough to be a prep school silver medalist wrestler.

It doesn't matter how little you start with. Anyone can ultimately prevail.

Mental toughness is even more important than physical strength. Everywhere you go, others are seeking power over you—individuals, corporations, nations (including your own government). The easiest way to exert power over someone else is to intimidate him. Those who prevail are not intimidated. Instead, the prevailer pays close attention to his would-be intimidator, studying his method and technique. Why? Because the would-be intimidator invariably uses a technique by which he himself can be intimidated. By studying the tactics of his antagonist, the prevailer can apply psychological jujitsu and turn that technique back upon his opponent.

An example of what I mean by psychological jujitsu occurred during my confinement in the Danbury, Connecticut, medium-security prison. One of the staff, a steward in the kitchen, was a native German who had as a young boy been a member of the Hitler Youth, an organization to which young boys in Nazi Germany belonged if their parents knew what was good for them. In the same prison was another, older German native, Arno Witt, who was a prisoner rather than a member of the staff.

One day in the mess hall, Witt helped himself to more food than the steward thought was his fair share, and, to intimidate him, the steward berated him in German in front of the other prisoners. Witt did not reply, biding his time. He had learned, however, that the steward thought being chastised in German before the American prisoners was intimidating.

The stewards had instituted an "ethnic meal" program; we had, for example, Mexican night (tacos and burritos) and Italian night (spaghetti and meatballs). One day, the German steward put on a German night, with wurst and sauerbraten. It was awful. When the steward came out to see how his efforts were being received, the American prisoners booed and made loud remarks like "No wonder youse lost da war!"

Arno Witt saw his chance.

What the German steward did not know was that Herr Witt had been a *fallschirmjäger,* a paratrooper, in the Wehrmacht during World War II, and, moreover, an officer, an *oberleutnaut.* When the steward came down the aisle in the mess hall, Witt jumped out in front of him and snapped a commanding *"Achtung!"* Instinctively, the steward snapped to a brace, whereupon former *oberleutnaut* Witt chewed him out unmercifully in German. I could understand a good bit of it—something about how the food on the Eastern Front in Russia during the winter was better. But the real crusher came at the end, reducing the steward to tears as he turned and fled back to the kitchen, when Witt told him he was "a disgrace to the Reich and the Führer!"

FAILURE: THE GREAT INSTRUCTOR

One intimidates a person, of course, by scaring him. As the great eighteenth-century British parliamentarian Edmund Burke noted,

"No passion so effectively robs the mind of all its powers of acting and reasoning as fear." Burke was right: fear is paralyzing. And the single most paralyzing form of fear is self-generated—the fear of *failure.* But select anyone who is successful and go back to the time *before* that person was acclaimed a "success." I guarantee you will find failure after failure after failure. Why? Because *failure instructs,* if you permit it to do so.

Every one of us is on the path to success. The problem is that so many of us step off the path before we ever arrive at our destination. Rid yourself of the fear of failure. After all, if you fail, you at least learn what not to do. Accept that instruction and try another way.

Of course, it is difficult to follow this dictum in practice. To stay on the path to success takes resolve and persistence. A classic example of learning through failure and achieving success through determination is the late George V. Higgins, the famous novelist and my good friend. Higgins is recognized as a master of American dialogue. If you haven't read him, it's akin to not having read Mark Twain. He burst on the scene of American letters in 1972 with a masterpiece called *The Friends of Eddie Coyle* and went on from there to a splendid career that was cut short by his untimely death in 1999.

I got to know George at the height of the Watergate scandal. He was one of the few people with the courage to come to my assistance at a time when I was about as popular as a child-molesting member of the Ku Klux Klan charged with matricide and arson of an orphanage. A lifelong Democrat, he had an unimpeachable sense of right and wrong, and he was instrumental in getting President Carter to commute my 21.5-year sentence (for the Watergate break-in and refusing to rat on my fellow conspirators, including the archetypal rodent, John Dean). After my release from prison—I ended up serving a little longer than we were in World War II—I set out to write a novel (what became *Out of Control,* published in 1979 by St. Martin's Press), and so I asked George how he had gotten his start. While working as a prosecutor to support his family, he said, he sat at the kitchen table every night and weekend and wrote. The first book he completed was rejected by every publisher to which he sent it. So he sought and received criticism to improve his next effort, he said, then tried again.

After he told me this, I looked at Higgins with new respect. But I still had no real idea of his determination. "How many books did you write before the first one was published?" I asked.

"Fourteen."

"Fourteen?"

"Fourteen."

George V. Higgins, the young lawyer who was proclaimed an "overnight success" with *The Friends of Eddie Coyle,* had sat down at his kitchen table every night after a full day's work as a prosecutor and written fourteen novels—and had experienced fourteen rejections. He failed again and again and again, but he did not stop working. Now, there's a man with resolve. There's a man with persistence. There's a man who made failure work for him as a teacher.

A key element of the fear of failure is concern for what others will think of you if you fail at something. It's one thing to fall flat on your face when there are no witnesses. You just get up, dust yourself off, and go on without giving it another thought. It is quite another thing to fall on your face on the dance floor at the prom after cutting in on the Homecoming Queen. Everyone laughs at you. Simply put, however, those who prevail don't care. They understand the important distinction between *character* and *reputation*.

CHARACTER

Reputation, by definition, is what others think of you. That is not in your control. I could go to your hometown and spend two weeks spreading a vicious falsehood about you. Even if the rumor I spread had no basis in fact whatsoever, chances are that some people would believe it. That is just human nature, and the law of averages. There's nothing you can do about that. In fact, the more righteously you have tried to live your life, the more some people will *want* to believe it. ("I just knew it, Agnes. There she is, every Sunday in church, and all the while . . . !")

Those who prevail know they cannot control what others think of them and don't waste their time trying. Instead, they invest their psychic energy in *character*. Character is what you really are—or as Heraclitus put it circa 500 B.C., "Character is destiny"—and it is 100 percent within your control.

Character is formed, for good or ill, by the choices a person habitually makes. Those who habitually take morally good decisions build good character. Those who habitually take bad moral decisions build bad character. The prevailers have a formula:

"What you think about, you do. What you do, you become."
Character *is* destiny.

Here are two examples: A young man with a flair for mathematics takes a job as a bank teller. Behind the counter he sees a river of currency flowing by, and it occurs to him that despite all of the bank's internal controls and the bank examiners' regular inspection procedures, he could devise a way to skim off some of the currency for himself with no one ever the wiser. So he thinks and he thinks and he thinks, and one day, as he's showering, it comes to him: *Yes!* Then he does it. And what does he become? A thief.

Now consider a girl raised in comfort in a spacious home. Even as a teenager she notices the plight of the needy and wonders what she can do to help them. It occurs to her that if she thinks about this problem long enough and prays about it, she might be able to come up with something to alleviate the suffering. So she thinks and she thinks and she prays and she prays, and finally it strikes her—she will devote her life to helping the destitute. She will live among them and make a real difference in countless lives. What does she become? Mother Teresa.

What you think about, you do. What you do, you become. Those who prevail understand that.

ACHIEVING REAL GOALS

Mere survivors know of the importance of setting goals and working to achieve them. One of the secrets of the prevailers is that they understand the critical distinction between *real* goals and merely *apparent* ones.

My experience in prison reinforced the importance of recognizing this difference. At one point during my imprisonment, I was approached by an elderly, distinguished-looking man of Italian extraction. The U.S. government had accused this gentleman of being more organized than it likes people to be. He and some other prisoners came to me with a request: "Liddy, we got a bad hack here and we wanna whack him, and the woid on the yard is, you used to hit for Uncle, and we wanna tap into your expoitese, here." A "hack" is a guard and to "hit" is to kill. "Uncle" means the federal government. A "bad" guard is someone dangerous.

And this guard was indeed dangerous. Just before I had been transferred back to this particular prison, there had been a fire in the cell block. As the flames raged, a prisoner went to the special telephone that the guards used to communicate with Control, which was manned twenty-four hours a day. When the guard on duty at Control answered the phone, the prisoner exclaimed, "We got a bad fire here! Send for the fire engines!" But all the guard said was, "Inmates ain't allowed to use this phone." Then he hung up. The prisoners called Control five times, and five times the guard hung up on them. Five prisoners burned to death. That's what is meant by a bad guard.

Still, one replies very carefully to a request for a hit. Although I was well into my forties and still had nearly two decades remaining on my sentence, I knew that one day I'd be free again. Yet I also understood the position of my associates, who knew they were going to spend the rest of their lives in prison and could not tolerate a bad guard. So I told them, "Gentlemen, I appreciate the trust and confidence in me implicit in your request, and without getting into any classified matters I may or may not have engaged in for our government, let me say that, with all due respect, I think you're confusing a real goal with a merely apparent one."

After a long pause, the leader said, "Uh...run that by us again?"

"Look," I said, "what you really want to do is neutralize this guy so that he can never be a problem again."

His face lit up. "Yeah," he replied enthusiastically, "we're gonna kill him. That'll neutralize him!"

"You still don't understand. They get unhappy when you kill one of them. They have their ways of expressing that unhappiness. The food, which is already nothing to write home about, will get decidedly worse and will be in short supply. Winter is coming. When your wives, children, and grandchildren come to visit on Sundays, I guarantee there will be no heat in the visiting room. They'll freeze and get pneumonia. The winter clothing will disappear, and you'll freeze, too."

"Okay, okay, so what's your great idea?"

"You give me your complete cooperation, and if we don't neutralize him in thirty days, then we'll do it your way."

By that time I knew prisons extremely well, and I recognized the advantages we the prisoners had over the guards. Though convicts often lack formal education, they are for the most part shrewd, cunning, aggressive personalities. It is not the shy and retiring sort who walks into the First National Bank with a pistol in his hand and tells twenty people, "Face down, on the floor!"

How about the guards? Well, who would voluntarily put himself in prison for thirty years? The short answer is someone who wanted very much to become a police officer—and failed. Don't ever let anyone tell you that a prison guard is a law enforcement officer. Either he couldn't get into the police academy because he was too stupid and uneducated, or having gotten in through connections, he flunked out or shot himself (or someone else) in the ass on the firing range. Next, he decided that with law enforcement out of the question, he'd become a fireman. But he kept setting fire to himself, and once the fire department understood that he was dangerous to the lives of other firemen, that occupation, too, was denied him. He couldn't go home to the family farm because he kept destroying expensive farm machinery, which was why he had to leave home to begin with—after failing out of high school because even the remedial program couldn't teach him to read and write. So the male village idiot marries the female or, if he's lucky, persuades the local Bride of Frankenstein, who *can* read and write, but from whose face lepers recoil in horror, to accept him. Desperate for some way to feed the poor wretch, he voluntarily puts himself in prison for thirty years and becomes a prison guard.

So therein lay our advantage. Whereas the prisoners, illiterate or not, were physically and psychologically strong, shrewd, and cunning, the guards, literate or not, were psychologically weak, dull, and dense. The mentally impoverished guard force anticipated opposition from the prisoners, but they were only trained to resist *physical* opposition. Violence, therefore, was the last thing I would counsel.

The bad guard we were targeting was one of the functional illiterates on the guard force. He was a big, fat, ugly guy who had a big, fat, ugly wife, though she was *not* illiterate. Quite the contrary, she was a stenographer who worked in the prison's administrative offices. I knew this guard's weakness. He was an insanely jealous husband. That may seem odd, given my description of his wife, but remember, to a rhinoceros, another rhino is gorgeous. The guard believed that because his wife was literate and working in administration with the other literates— a whole evolutionary class above him—she would be attracted to them and they to her. He feared he was being cuckolded.

How did I know that? The answer to that question requires what in Hollywood is called a "back story." When I first arrived at this prison, I found there an associate warden with a particularly foul reputation as to how he treated convicts. I don't believe in being a victim, however. No one can make you a victim. You have to accept victimhood. I never have and never shall. So I made an appointment to meet this man. Of course, he brought along his boss, the warden. I said to them, "Look, neither of you has anything to do with why I am here. I'm here because of an occupational hazard. You don't bother me, I won't bother you, and we'll get along fine." They didn't listen. They bothered me. Bad career move.

I decided to act. My first move was, in armed forces jargon, to get "intel." I wiretapped the prison's telephone system for about ninety days. It really wasn't hard. Every job in a prison is done with convict labor—always, of course, with some functional illiterate standing around supervising—so I just had a convict on the telephone-repair detail slip me the device I needed. Using what telephone repairmen call the "buttinsky"—a handset with a dial on the inside of the handle and two wires ending in alligator clips extending from one end—I listened to any conversation I wanted. That's how I found out how this particular guard felt about his wife.

The rest was easy. We planted little notes, knowing that, though he couldn't read them, he would get a trusted friend to tell him what they said. Within a week we had confirmed his worst suspicions—his wife was making it with every male employee in the joint. He set out immediately to trap her in her utterly nonexistent adultery. Any man who saw this woman approaching would flee, of course, but our notes had convinced the guard that his wife was cheating on him. Utterly frustrated, mad with jealousy, he quickly suffered a breakdown of what little mind he had and ended up at a funny farm. Now, that may sound cruel, but he was still alive. There were no repercussions. Real goal, versus merely apparent goal, achieved.

New Solutions for Old Problems

We all have problems—problems in our family lives, our business lives, our community lives, and, God knows, our national lives. Those who prevail face the same problems we all do. The difference between the survivor and the prevailer is in how each sets about *solving* problems.

When one seeks help with problems, one is inevitably offered what was called, when I was in the Army, the "school solution." In other words, one is referred to "the manual," which lists all the problems one might expect to run into and the relevant solutions. I saw how true this was when I worked for such large organizations as the U.S. Army, the FBI, and the Treasury Department, and it is the same way at places like General Motors, IBM, Exxon, and CBS. *Just consult the manual; it's right there in Section Five at Tab E.*

There's only one problem with the manual approach: Everybody has a copy of the manual. Everybody with the same problem arrives at Tab E. Everyone is doing the same thing, but it doesn't work anymore. The solution is out of date.

The people who prevail never consult the manual. They are creative in solving problems. They come up with *new* solutions.

Again, my experience in the tough world of prison drove home the significance of this point. When one first arrives at a prison, whether from another prison or "the street" (the outside world), one is never allowed into the general population. Rather, one is placed in something usually called the Classification Unit, or Orientation, along with all the other new guys. The guards claim that this is to test the prisoner, to determine whether he is better suited to stamp out white license plates with black numbers or black license plates with white numbers. But the real reason for the ninety-day quarantine is that prison officials have to determine whether the new prisoners are sick—for in a closed environment like a prison, disease can run rampant.

During my "Orientation," ninety-five other men and I were crammed into a place designed for fifty prisoners. Prison officials solved the sleeping problem with triple-decker bunks, but they could do nothing about fixed facilities—sinks, toilets, and showerheads. That led, after breakfast every morning, to incidents of social Darwinism. Everyone had to use the toilets at the same time, and the "school solution" for that problem was to have a fistfight over a toilet. The biggest, toughest guy got to use the toilet first; Caspar Milquetoast would get there at about two in the afternoon, long after he'd had a laundry problem. Fortunately for me, during my misspent youth in the service of our country, I had learned how to do some very damaging things to the soft parts of others' bodies with the hard parts of mine. "But," I said to myself, "that's the school solution. That's what the manual says at Tab E." Besides, the aesthetics of it were not appealing—having a fistfight over a toilet.

The better solution? I let the authorities know that I knew how to type. In a community where 50 percent of the population is functionally illiterate, the ability to type is an awe-inspiring skill. I was promptly raised to the high office of clerk of the unit, which gave me access to the two things I needed to solve my problem with the fixed facilities: a battered old Remington Standard typewriter and a supply of blank forms used for memoranda, something familiar to anyone who has ever worked for the federal government. I immediately cranked a stolen "optional form No. 10" into the old Remington and typed out a bureaucratic memorandum. Who better to create a bureaucratic memo than a veteran of work in Washington, D.C.?

United States Government
MEMORANDUM

To: All Concerned

From: Associate Warden, Operations

Subject: Venereal Disease Rate, Orientation Unit

There has been an alarming rate of increase of venereal disease in the Orientation Unit, particularly syphilis and gonorrhea. This trend must be reversed.

Action:

1. One each toilet will be set aside immediately for the exclusive use of those suffering from venereal disease.

2. A sign will be prepared and placed over said toilet which reads: 'VD ONLY'

3. This memorandum will be posted on the bulletin board in the Orientation Unit.

FOR THE WARDEN:

Signed: _____

I forged the associate warden's signature (another little talent I picked up in the service of our country), posted the memo on the bulletin board, and taped a "VD ONLY" sign over a commode. The next morning, I had my own private toilet. Now, it affected my reputation adversely. "Do you know what Liddy's got? I bet Nixon's got it too. I bet they all had it down there!" But what did I care? I had what I wanted.

SELF-RELIANCE

By now you have probably noticed a theme that unites all the traits of the prevailer: self-reliance. Those who prevail know that the best way to succeed in life is to take responsibility for what they are doing. If you want to prevail, only you can choose to use reason rather than be guided by emotion and instinct, to be physically and mentally strong, to take the right decisions and not be concerned about what others might think of you, to set real goals and not let fear of failure stop you from achieving them, to come up with the best solutions for the problems you face. No one else can do this for you.

Prevailers recognize that self-reliance applies to their spiritual natures, as well. Those who prevail in life, no matter their religion—Christian, Jew, Muslim, what have you—understand that we human beings are finite, while God is an infinite being. It is illogical to believe that the finite can comprehend the infinite, so they do not try to understand God. They recognize that God is to be praised, worshiped, loved, and obeyed, to the extent one can figure out His wishes by listening to one's conscience, but *not* understood.

With that in mind, those who prevail avoid the trap into which so many fall: praying to God to help them in situations that only the individual can control. Why, for instance, would God answer a prayer from a General Motors executive asking, "God, please help us to take 10 percent market share from Ford"? Are the employees of GM more righteous that those at Ford? Of course not. Abraham Lincoln recognized this during the Civil War, when, during his Second Inaugural Address, he observed, "Both [North and South] read the same Bible and pray to the same God, and each invokes His aid against the other." The war, Lincoln knew, could only be decided on the battlefield—by men, not God.

Those who prevail go to work to earn what they want and leave God out of it.

Looking Back, Looking Ahead: We Can Prevail

Throughout this book I have detailed the problems that have been taking root in this country in recent generations. With all these problems—all the assaults on our liberties, the failure of our education system, the difficulties with our military, and so much more—you might well throw up your hands and simply lament the changes this country is enduring.

But then you would be a mere survivor.

When I was a kid, this was a free country, and a great country. Men like Frank Smith and Joe Foss made sure of that. America can and will be great again, as long as we have the determination to face down those who would see America decline. It can happen. We can fix the mess of an education system we have, particularly if parents assume what is their moral responsibility for their own children's education. We can make the U.S. military as great as it was when we defeated Hitler's Wehrmacht and Hirohito's forces. We can halt the assaults on our liberties by becoming educated about what is really happening and standing up for our inalienable rights. It is up to you and me.

We can prevail, if we have the necessary *will*.

Appendix

THE KEY TO WATERGATE

WHEN I WAS A KID AND THIS WAS A FREE COUNTRY, we were free to debate our country's history. Because of the frantic efforts of the notorious rat John Dean, we almost lost that right.

The second Watergate burglary (the one detected by a watchman and the Washington, D.C., police) was committed on the night of 16–17 June 1972. It was one of the central political events of the twentieth century and led to the first resignation of an American president, Richard M. Nixon. I directed that burglary, believing that I was acting for the attorney general of the United States, John Mitchell, and, through him, the president, to seek political intelligence from the office of the chairman of the Democratic National Committee, Lawrence O'Brien. I was wrong. So were the United States Senate Select Committee on Watergate, the press (particularly the *Washington Post* and Messrs. Woodward and Bernstein), and the television network news organizations of NBC, ABC, and CBS. The self-contradicting testimony of John Dean, former counsel to President Nixon, deceived all as he betrayed his client to save his own worthless skin.

Dean and I have something in common from the point of view of historians. We are both what they call primary sources—actual participants in the events being recounted by the historians. Primary sources' accounts of events are given much greater weight than those of secondary sources. Secondary sources are the works of those who write or speak of the events as a result of studying the primary sources—contemporary newspaper reportage, for example, or the books produced by historians. John Dean wrote a book about Watergate, and for years it was used as a primary source. Not anymore. Here's why:

Dean's book was called *Blind Ambition*. When it was published, in 1976, he started it with the following "Author's Note":

> This book is a portrait—not a black-and-white photograph—of five years of my life. It represents my best effort to paint what I saw and reproduce what I heard. I have included detail, texture, tone, to make this history more vivid—though, I trust, no prettier. *I prepared for the writing of* Blind Ambition *the same way I prepared to testify before the Ervin Committee, before the special prosecutors, and in the cover-up trial.* But in the book I have included dialogue and enclosed it in quotation marks, whereas in my testimony I deliberately refrained from dramatizing the events I was relating.
>
> While many White House conversations were taped, many were not. To reconstruct what occurred, I reviewed an enormous number of documents as well as my own testimony. Wherever possible, I spoke to others who

were present with me during discussions, or I talked to people to whom I'd related conversations shortly after they took place, and I referred to notes I had kept. I have also, of course, relied on my memory in this account of my experiences in the White House, and *while I do not claim to report the dialogues verbatim, I vouch for their essential accuracy. To borrow my lawyer's phrase: "I'm ready to get on the box"*—take a lie-detector test.

A final matter of importance. I have often read authors' acknowledgments, but I never before quite realized what they were saying. Now I do, and it is not merely a gesture when I offer thanks to all those who helped with this book. I sincerely thank Marcia Nassiter and David Obst for their early encouragement; Estelle Oppenheim and Marie Ralphs for typing and retyping many drafts; Patty Firestone and Hays Gorey for critical readings and helpful suggestions; Richard Snyder, Sophie Sorkin, Vera Schneider, Harriet Ripinsky, David Nettles, Frank Metz, Joanna Ekman and the staff of Simon and Schuster for their enthusiastic and professional support; *Taylor Branch for his talented assistance and patient tutoring;* and Alice Mayhew, my editor, for guiding—more truly, forcefully but thoroughly driving—the book to completion [emphasis added].

Notice that in his author's note Dean stated, "I prepared for the writing of *Blind Ambition* the same way I prepared to testify before the Ervin Committee, before the special prosecutors, and in the cover-up trial." That "while I do not claim to report the dialogues verbatim, I vouch for their essential accuracy." And that "'I'm ready to get on the box'—take a lie-detector test." Finally, he said, "I sincerely thank...Taylor Branch for his talented assistance and patient tutoring." Those statements were made, of course, back in 1976, before Dean's contradictions of himself had been discovered and when, obviously, he believed they never would be.

In 1991, however, a book entitled *Silent Coup* was published. It contained a lengthy section entitled "Golden Boy," a reference to John Dean, which demonstrated that when Dean testified in different venues about the same events, he was inconsistent and contradictory, and that when he wrote about the same events in *Blind Ambition,* he continued the same practice. It wasn't Dean's version versus that of someone else; it was Dean versus Dean.

After intensive investigation into the facts, I publicly endorsed *Silent Coup* on my nationally syndicated radio program and dared Dean to sue me for defamation. I did so because I wanted a public trial to demonstrate to the entire world that Dean cannot be trusted to tell the truth. Dean finally sued me in 1992. According to the complaint, Dean claimed he was defamed by statements which conveyed that Dean "was guilty of criminal conduct in planning, aiding, abetting and directing the Watergate break-ins, and gave perjured testimony under oath in violation of the law with catastrophic consequences to alleged innocent persons, was a traitor to his nation as was Benedict Arnold, and that all expressions of constitution and historical writings by John Dean since his testimony at the Watergate hearings and trials have been and are a self serving, ongoing histori-cal fraud."

Dean's process server came to the studio from which I was broadcasting and served me live, on the air. I asked him how much he thought the papers weighed and he answered, "About two pounds." I said, "Good, because I'm going to shove them up Dean's ass." Figuratively, that's just what I did.

In a civil suit, each side gets to "depose" (interrogate under oath) the other side. After a lot more investigation, which led to the uncovering of the *real* reason behind the Watergate break-in, my lawyers, John B. Williams and Kerrie L. Hook, partners of the crack Washington, D.C., law firm of Collier Shannon Scott, assisted by my son Tom Liddy, then of the same law firm and a former United States Marine Corps captain of infantry, grilled Dean under oath and broke him.

Remember all those things Dean said about *Blind Ambition*? How he had prepared to write it? How he was willing to take a lie-detector test about what he wrote in it? Well, guess what? Under oath Dean was forced to admit that not only did he not write *Blind Ambition,* he didn't even fully *read it* before it was pub-lished! He admitted that *Blind Ambition* was actually written by a ghostwriter named Taylor Branch, and he claimed that the errors in it, the falsity, were put there by Branch. Passage after passage, according to Dean, was "pure Taylor Branch" or "made up out of whole cloth by Taylor Branch." Now, I don't believe that any more than I would believe anything else John Dean says. Taylor Branch is not some obscure nonentity trying to earn a buck as a ghost for a disgraced lawyer who can't write. I know Taylor

Branch. He is a Pulitzer Prize–winning author who was the editor of *Harper's* when I wrote a piece for that highly regarded
magazine. He denies making anything up in the book he wrote
for Dean, and I believe him. His dealings with me were always
meticulously honest and highly professional.

Why, then, did Dean abandon *Blind Ambition* and make
such outlandish claims about the multitude of things in it that
are inconsistent with his Watergate testimony? *He had no choice.*
Apparently, it was easier to admit he didn't write *Blind Ambition*
and blame Taylor Branch for the errors in it than it would have
been to say he had lied to Watergate investigators.

Armed with Dean's deposition and masses of new facts
developed during years of investigation into what really happened at Watergate and why, I tried for eight years to get Dean
to trial. But Dean is like the kid who challenges you in the hall-
way to "meet me outside after school" to fight and then never
shows up. He's a coward. Finally, I cornered him—or so I
thought. The United States District Court judge called a pretrial
conference to discuss the order of proof to be presented at trial
and other matters. I was there, but Dean failed to show up. His
lawyers were there, but no Dean. Following Dean's instructions,
his lawyers withdrew most of his charges against me, and the
judge dismissed the rest. End of case? No.

Remember that Dean claimed that not only didn't he write
Blind Ambition, he didn't even fully read it? Wait until you hear
his explanation for *that* yarn. According to Dean, speaking under
oath, he was ill and in bed when he received the galley proofs of

Blind Ambition from the publisher, and his wife wouldn't let him review them to make corrections because he had once stained her sheets with ink from his pen. (Ever hear of that new high-tech invention called a pencil? *Hello!*) The point is that Dean, when cornered, hid behind his wife's skirts. It would not be the last time that Dean hid behind a woman, which is why I say the case was not yet closed.

On 2 April 1996, I delivered a speech at James Madison University in Harrisonburg, Virginia. The speech was a motivational one having nothing to do with Watergate. After the speech, as is my wont, I entertained an extensive question-and-answer session with the audience. One of the questions I was asked concerned Watergate, and I responded. The same thing occurred at a lecture I gave aboard a cruise ship in the Mediterranean Sea in August 1997, and I was asked a similar question on the radio on 25 April of the same year. As a result, a one-time secretary at the Democratic National Committee headquarters in the Watergate office building, Ida Maxwell "Maxie" Wells, also sued me for defamation.

Chief Judge J. Frederick Motz of the United States District Court in Baltimore, Maryland, described how the Wells suit came about: "This case had its origins in the *Dean* litigation. Wells's present counsel, who was then representing the Deans (but not her), attended the James Madison University event where Liddy was speaking and tape-recorded the allegedly defamatory remarks. He then transcribed those remarks and, apparently believing that it was in the Deans's [*sic*] interest to have parallel litigation instituted against Liddy, had a copy of the transcript sent to Wells and encouraged her to sue."

After being badgered for a year, the woman finally, on the last day she legally could, sued me. Whereupon the Deans' former lawyer became *her* lawyer. That's one way to get clients. It's called barratry. Having found another woman behind whose skirts to hide, Dean folded his suit against me, for my money so he wouldn't have to face a public trial at which his irreconcilable accounts of Watergate events would be exposed to the press and public. By the way, John Dean was noticed as a witness for Miss Wells at the trial of her lawsuit against me. To the surprise of no one who knows him, once again he didn't show up.

The vast amount of new information about Watergate that has been discovered during the massive investigations resulting from the nine-year lawsuit that the Deans withdrew before trial, and Miss Wells's five-year lawsuit, could easily justify an entirely new, and very thick, book. I, however, have but a chapter with which to bring you up to date and demonstrate that the conventional (i.e., the *Washington Post*) version of the scandal that rocked our nation is as wrong as a Flat Earth Society pamphlet. The most efficient way to do that is to show you the record. Read for yourself one court's description of Miss Wells's lawsuit and the facts set forth in *Silent Coup,* and then examine several key pieces of evidence:

A portion of the 28 July 1999 decision in the Ida Wells case from the United States Court of Appeals for the Fourth Circuit. *(14 pages)*

IDA MAXWELL WELLS, Plaintiff-Appellant, v. G. GORDON LIDDY, Defendant-Appellee, PHILLIP MACKIN BAILLEY, Movant.

No. 98-1962

UNITED STATES COURT OF APPEALS
FOR THE FOURTH CIRCUIT

March 3, 1999, Argued
July 28, 1999, Decided

JUDGES: Before WILKINS AND WILLIAMS, Circuit Judges, and LEE, United States District Judge for the Eastern District of Virginia, sitting by designation. Judge Williams wrote the opinion, in which Judge Wilkins and Judge Lee joined.

OPINION:
WILLIAMS, Circuit Judge:

Ida Maxwell "Maxie" Wells, who was a secretary at the Democratic National Committee (DNC) for a short time in 1972, filed a defamation action against G. Gordon Liddy stemming from his advocacy of an alternative theory explaining the purpose of the June 17, 1972, Watergate break-in. During several public appearances and on a world wide web site Liddy stated that the burglars' objective during the Watergate break-in was to determine whether the Democrats possessed information embarrassing to John Dean.[1] More specifically, Liddy asserted that the burglars were seeking a compromising photograph of Dean's fiance that was located in Wells's desk among several photographs that were used to offer prostitution services to out-of-town guests.

Upon Liddy's motion for summary judgment, the district court determined that Wells was an involuntary public figure who could not prove actual malice by clear and convincing evidence. Additionally, the district court determined that Louisiana law applied to all of Wells's defamation counts and that Louisiana law would require even a private figure to prove actual malice. On the basis of these rulings, the district court entered judgment in Liddy's favor. Because we determine that Wells is not a public figure for purposes of the ongoing public debate regarding Watergate and we also conclude that Louisiana law does not apply to two of Wells's defamation counts, we reverse the district court's grant of summary judgment and remand for further proceedings consistent with this opinion.

I.

In February of 1972, the then-twenty-three-year-old Wells moved from her hometown of Jackson, Mississippi to Washington, D.C. and began work at the DNC as the secretary to Spencer Oliver, Executive Director of the Association of State Democratic Chairmen. Wells continued in the employ of the DNC and Oliver until late July 1972. Throughout her employment, the DNC offices were located in the Watergate complex.

A few months after Wells started her job at the DNC, Frank Wills, a security guard, noticed a piece of tape propping

---

1.   John Dean was legal counsel to President Richard M. Nixon in
     1972.

open the door to the DNC offices while making his routine
rounds during the early morning hours of June 17, 1972. *See
David Behrens, "Day by Day," Newsday, June 17, 1992, at 63.*
Wills removed the tape. *See id.* When he made his next
scheduled rounds, however, the tape had been returned to the
doorway. *See id.* Suspecting that something was afoot, Wills
called the police. *See id.* Shortly thereafter, the police arrived
and apprehended five men: James W. McCord, Frank Sturgis,
Eugenio R. Martinez, Virgilio R. Gonzalez, and Bernard L.
Barker. *See Alfred E. Lewis, "Five Held in Plot to Bug Democrats'
Office Here," Wash. Post, June 18, 1972, at A1.* Of these five, one
was a recent CIA retiree, three were Cuban emigres, and the
fifth had trained Cuban exiles for possible guerrilla activity
after the failed Bay of Pigs invasion. *See id.* The men were
wearing business attire and surgical gloves. They were carrying $2,300 in sequentially numbered one hundred dollar bills,
sophisticated electronic surveillance equipment, lock picks,
door jimmies, one walkie-talkie, a short wave receiver, forty
rolls of thirty-five millimeter film, three pen-sized tear gas
guns, *see id.,* and the White House phone number of E. Howard
Hunt.[2] When initially asked about the events at the Watergate, White House spokesman Ronald Ziegler dismissed the
incident as "A third-rate burglary attempt." *Gaylord Shaw,
"Watergate Third Rate Burglary," Newsday, June 17, 1992, at 62.*

In the wake of the burglary, the FBI determined that
Spencer Oliver's telephone conversations were being elec-
tronically monitored from a listening post located in room 723

---

2. These well-chronicled facts regarding the June 17, 1972, Watergate break-in are not in dispute in the present appeal and are
   recited to provide information regarding Wells's alleged public
   participation at the time of the break-in and the historical context
   surrounding Wells's claims.

of the Howard Johnson's Motor Inn across the street from the Watergate. Because Wells often used Oliver's phone to make personal calls, some of her conversations were intercepted.[3] Additionally, a drawer of Wells's desk was opened during the break-in. As a result, she was questioned by the FBI. Although there is some factual dispute between the parties over whether the FBI informed Wells of the discovery, the FBI also determined that a key found in a burglar's possession fit the lock on Wells's desk.

In September of 1972, Wells was subpoenaed to appear as a witness before the federal grand jury investigating the break-in. On September 15, 1972, the grand jury indicted the five burglars as well as the two men who allegedly had coordinated the break-in, E. Howard Hunt, a White House aide, and G. Gordon Liddy, counsel for the Committee to Reelect the President. *"Watergate Chronology,"* News & Observer *(Raleigh, N.C.), June 17, 1992, at A4.* Appearing before Judge John Sirica in United States District Court for the District of Columbia in early January of 1973, the five Watergate burglars pleaded guilty to a variety of burglary, conspiracy, and wiretapping charges. *See John Berlau & Jennifer G. Hickey, "List of Jailbirds is Long, but Sentences are Short,"* Insight Mag., *June 23, 1997, at 10.* Each of the five burglars was sentenced to a prison term.[4] *See*

---

3. In 1972, *Newsweek* and the *International Herald-Tribune* reported that Wells's conversations had been intercepted. *Newsweek,* however, did not refer to Wells by name, but rather referred to her as Oliver's secretary.

4. Bernard Barker served twelve months in jail. *See "A Watergate Scorecard,"* Wall St. J., *Jan. 26, 1998, at A19.* Virgilio Gonzalez spent fifteen months in prison. *See id.* Eugenio Rolando Martinez also served fifteen months. *See id.* James McCord was incarcerated for four months, *see id.,* and Frank Sturgis was jailed for thirteen months, *see id.*

"A Watergate Scorecard," Wall St. J., *Jan. 26, 1998, at A19.* E. Howard Hunt also pleaded guilty to six counts of burglary, conspiracy, and wiretapping. *See Berlau & Hickey, supra.* As a result, he was imprisoned for thirty-three months. *See "A Watergate Scorecard," supra.* Liddy neither pleaded guilty nor cooperated with the prosecution. He was tried on multiple counts of burglary, conspiracy, and interception of wire and oral communications, was found guilty, and received a sentence of six to twenty years imprisonment. *See Berlau & Hickey, supra.* Liddy served fifty-two months in jail as a result of his convictions. *See "Watergate Scorecard," supra.*

Shortly after pleading guilty, James McCord wrote a letter from prison stating that he had been pressured to plead guilty and to lie during the district court proceedings relating to the Watergate incident. *See "Watergate Timeline,"* Cin. Enquirer, *June 17, 1997, at A6.* In his letter, McCord implicated John Dean, the president's counsel, and John Mitchell, the Attorney General, as the individuals who had been pressuring the Watergate burglars to withhold information. *See "Watergate TimeLine" (visited April 29, 1999), http://vcepolitics.com/wgate/timeline.htm.*

As a result of McCord's revelations implicating high level administration officials, in February of 1973 the United States Senate voted (77-0) to establish a Select Committee on Presidential Campaign Activities to be chaired by Senator Sam Ervin of North Carolina. *See id.* Wells, who had by this time relocated to Atlanta, Georgia, returned to Washington on June 20, 1974 to testify before the Committee. Wells's testimony was not part of the televised Watergate hearings. During its investigation, the Senate Committee discovered a campaign of political "dirty tricks" of which the Watergate break-in was a part. The White House's effort to cover up its involvement led to the imprisonment of several high ranking White House officials and ultimately to the resignation of President Nixon in August of 1974.

Wells returned to Washington in 1976 and served as a secretary to President Carter. After she left that post, she entered a Ph.D. program in English at Louisiana State University and at the time of this lawsuit planned to pursue a career as a college professor. Liddy was released from prison in 1977, and since that time he has become a successful radio talk show personality. He has also published his autobiography, *Will,* and is a frequent speaker on the lecture circuit.

In 1991, Len Colodny and Robert Gettlin authored a book entitled *Silent Coup: The Removal of a President. Len Colodny & Robert Gettlin,* Silent Coup: The Removal of a President *(1991).* In *Silent Coup,* Colodny and Gettlin discussed new evidence regarding the Watergate break-in and concluded that the purpose of the break-in was not simply to replace a malfunctioning listening device that had been installed in an earlier break-in at the DNC in May 1972.[5] Rather, Colodny and Gettlin concluded that John Dean had personally authorized the Watergate break-in to protect his own reputation and the reputation of his now-wife, Maureen Biner.[6]

---

5. This is the majority or conventional view of the purpose for the June 17, 1972, Watergate break-in. *See, e.g., Karlyn Barker & Walter Pincus, "Watergate Revisited,"* Wash. Post, *June 14, 1992, at A1.*

6. The Deans filed a libel suit against Colodny, Gettlin, Liddy and *Silent Coup*'s publisher, St. Martin's Press, in the United States District Court for the District of Columbia. The Deans have settled with St. Martin's Press. *See George Lardner Jr., "Watergate Libel Suit Settled,"* Wash. Post, *July 23, 1997, at C1.* The suit against Colodny, Gettlin, and Liddy is still pending. Wells is not a party to the Deans' suit.

In *Silent Coup,* Colodny and Gettlin assert that an attorney, Phillip Mackin Bailley, assisted a woman named Erica L. "Heidi" Rikan expand her preexisting call-girl operation located at the Columbia Plaza apartments, near the Watergate, by promoting Rikan's services to Bailley's DNC connections. The book also notes that Maureen Biner was a close friend of Rikan. According to *Silent Coup,* when Bailley came to visit the DNC, he asked for Spencer Oliver, but because Oliver was out of the office at the time, his secretary, Wells, gave him a tour of the DNC facilities. As a result of Bailley's contact with the DNC, *Silent Coup* reports that one client per day was referred to Rikan from DNC headquarters. Colodny and Gettlin state that meetings with call girls were arranged on Oliver's phone while he was out of the office, and that Oliver's telephone was the target of the first, May 1972, Watergate break-in during which the wiretaps were initially installed. According to *Silent Coup* Bailley was eventually arrested and indicted for violations of the Mann Act (transporting under-age females across state lines for immoral purposes), extortion, blackmail, pandering, and procuring. As a result, Bailley's address books were seized. *Silent Coup* also notes that Maureen Biner's name appeared in Bailley's address books.

After news of Bailley's arrest appeared in the newspaper, together with information regarding a Capitol Hill call-girl ring staffed by secretaries, office workers, and a White House secretary, *Silent Coup* reports that John Dean called the Assistant United States Attorney investigating the Bailley case and summoned him to the White House. During the meeting, Dean reportedly told the Assistant United States Attorney that he thought the Democrats had leaked the prostitution ring story. Thereafter, Dean made a photocopy of Bailley's address books and proceeded to compare the names from the book to a list of White House staff. Colodny and Gettlin state that Dean immediately would have recognized Maureen Biner's name as well as the alias of her good friend Rikan during this examination.

The implication of Colodny and Gettlin's narrative is that the June 17, 1972, Watergate break-in was ordered by Dean so that he could determine whether the Democrats had information linking Maureen Biner to the Bailley/Rikan call-girl ring and whether they planned to use such information to embarrass him. After the break-in was ordered, Alfred Baldwin, the man who was operating the listening post at the Howard Johnson's motel, visited DNC headquarters in order to "case" the layout of the offices. Because he posed as a friend of Oliver to gain admittance to the office, he was referred by the receptionist to Wells, who gave him a tour of the facility. During the visit, *Silent Coup* concludes "Baldwin either somehow obtained a key from Wells, or stole one." *Colodny & Gettlin, supra at 149*. Colodny and Gettlin contend that the purloined key was found on Watergate burglar Martinez. Although *Silent Coup* posits the question, "Why would a Watergate burglar have a key to Wells's desk in his possession and what items of possible interest to a Watergate burglar were maintained in Wells's locked desk drawer?" *id. at 159,* the book never proffers a specific answer.[7]

---

7. *Silent Coup* is not the first book on Watergate in which the DNC is
    linked to prostitution activities. The first mention of prostitution
    occurred in 1976 in J. Anthony Lukas's book *Nightmare: The Under-
    side of the Nixon Years. Nightmare* noted that conversations inter-
    cepted by Baldwin at the Howard Johnson's listening post were
    of an intimate personal nature and led to unconfirmed rumors
    that Oliver's phone was being used for a call-girl service for high-
    ranking dignitaries. *See J. Anthony Lukas,* Nightmare: The Under-

Liddy had extensive conversations with Colodny regarding the theory of the break-in promulgated in *Silent Coup* beginning in 1988. By 1991, Liddy had reached the conclusion that Colodny and Gettlin's theory was correct. As a result, in 1991 Liddy published a special paperback edition of his autobiography *Will* that included a discussion and endorsement of the *Silent Coup* theory. On June 3, 1991, Liddy had a meeting with Phillip Mackin Bailley, during which Bailley discussed his involvement with the Rikan prostitution ring. During the meeting, Bailley told Liddy that tasteful photographs of the

---

side of the Nixon Years *201 (1976)*. In 1984, a second book was published in which the call-girl ring theory surfaced. In *Secret Agenda: Watergate, Deep Throat and the FBI,* author Jim Hougan specifically mentioned the Columbia Plaza prostitution ring and Phillip Bailley. *See Jim Hougan,* Secret Agenda: Watergate, Deep Throat and the FBI *178 (1984).* In his book, however, Hougan asserts that the CIA, through its ex-officer E. Howard Hunt, was secretly manipulating the activities leading to the Watergate break-in. *See id. at 126.* Additionally, *Secret Agenda* also concluded that the timing of the Watergate break-in was influenced by Bailley's arrest. *See id. at 173–74.* Finally, *Secret Agenda* first revealed that Wells's key was in the possession of Martinez during the burglary. *See id. at 173.* Lukas wrote a review of *Secret Agenda* for the *New York Times* in November of 1984 in which he noted, "Hougan... suggests that the tap...was indeed intercepting conversations on Mr. Oliver's phone because a D.N.C. secretary was using the phone to introduce visiting Democrats [to a prostitute]. Mr. Hougan does not identify the secretary at this point, but later strongly suggests that it was Ida 'Maxie' Wells, Mr. Oliver's personal secretary." *(J.A. at 405.)* Wells requested that the *Times* retract or correct the book review to remove references to her connection to the call-girl ring. The request was refused. Thereafter, Wells wrote a letter to the editor stating "at no time did I know anything about any link to any call girl operation and at no time did I have any involvement in or to any call girl operation." *(J.A. at 490.)*

Rikan call-girls wearing see-through negligees were kept in a desk at the DNC in the Oliver/Wells/Governors area. According to Bailley, various personnel at the DNC would show the photos to DNC visitors and would arrange rendezvous. Bailley also stated that several DNC employees were compensated for making referrals.

After he reissued his autobiography, Liddy began routinely incorporating Colodny and Gettlin's *Silent Coup* theory, including the additional information garnered from Bailley, into his public speeches. He would do so either by informing the listeners of the recent developments in the Watergate case as part of his prepared remarks or in response to questions raised by audience members during a question-and-answer period at the end of the program. Several of Liddy's public appearances during which he presented this theory are the subject of Wells's defamation suit. He delivered one such speech at James Madison University in Harrisonburg, Virginia on April 2, 1996 (JMU speech).

During the JMU speech, an audience member asked Liddy:

> Mr. Liddy, I have a question...I want your in put [*sic*] on one of the theories surrounding the mystery of Watergate. It specifically related to James McCord. There are some who believe that maybe he wasn't working along with you, he had ulterior motives. And what gives...credit to this theory is that an ex-CIA agent...made two critical mistakes that really... caused you all to be caught. What do you think about that? (*J.A. at 996.*)

In response to the question, Liddy began to explain the *Silent Coup* theory of Watergate to the audience. During the explanation, he noted that the Howard Johnson's listening post "looked directly down at a desk of a secretary named Maxine Wells, and her telephone. And they had a telescopic lens camera pointed at that. And that is where the wiretap was subsequently found by the democrats on that phone." *(J.A. at 998.)* After explaining the Bailley/Rikan prostitution ring and Maureen Biner's connection to the ring, Liddy stated:

> Some members of the DNC were using the call girl ring as an asset to entertain visiting firemen. And to that end they had a manila envelope that you could open or close by wrapping a string around a wafer. And in that envelope were twelve photographs of an assortment of these girls and then one group photograph of them. And what you see is what you get. It was kept he said in that desk of Ida Maxine Wells. Thus, the camera [and] all the rest of it. And what they were doing is as these people would be looking at the brochure, if you want to call it that, and making the telephone call to arrange the assignation that was being wiretapped, recorded and photographed. *(J.A. at 998–99.)*

Liddy gave a similar speech while on a Mediterranean cruise (cruise ship speech) in August 1997.[8] Liddy also discussed Watergate during an appearance on the *Don and Mike* radio show on April 25, 1997. During the *Don and Mike* broadcast, Don's son Bart, who was doing research for a school project, asked Liddy questions about Watergate:

---

8. The cruise ship speech was never transcribed.

Bart: I was wondering what was your role in the Water gate breakup [*sic*] scandal?

Liddy: Okay. I was the political intelligence chieftain, as well as the general counsel of the Committee to Reelect the President.... Now what I did not know is that John Dean did not trust me any more than I trusted him. And so my men were told, although I was not, that they were to go in there and, what, the telephone that was wired was not Mr. O'Brien's but was the telephone that was on the desk of a woman named ... Ida Maxwell Wells ... and she was the secretary to a man named R. Spencer Oliver.

. . . .

Liddy: Well next door to the Watergate was a place called the Columbia Plaza Apartments and operating in there was what is known as a call girl ring and the lawyer who represented those girls was arrested by the FBI and they found his address book that had the names of his clients and also that included the call girl and there was a woman in there whose code name was "Clout."

. . . .

Liddy: Now to make a long story short. That was kind of what it was all about and if you want a secondary source on Watergate, you know to read about what was going on and everything. There is a book called *Silent Coup.* (*J.A. at 1021, 1022, 1023.*)

The fact of Liddy's belief in the Colodny and Gettlin Watergate theory also appeared on the Accuracy in Media site on the world wide web[9] in a review of the Oliver Stone directed film *Nixon.* Nixon *(Cinergi, Hollywood Pictures, Illusion Entertainment 1995).* The Accuracy in Media review criticized Stone for failing to seize an opportunity to adopt the *Silent Coup* theory of the Watergate break-in and for speculating that the Watergate burglars were looking for information linking Nixon to the Bay of Pigs invasion and the assassination of President Kennedy. In support of its argument that Stone should have pursued the *Silent Coup* theory, the web site characterized the theory as plausible and provided Liddy's explanation of the value of the *Silent Coup* theory:

> Not until Colodny and Gettlin wrote *Silent Coup* did Liddy realize that the true objective of this second raid was to get into the desk of Maxie Wells, Spencer Oliver's secretary, said to be the key figure in arranging dates with the call girls. Unknown to Liddy at the time, one of the burglars carried a key to Wells'[s] desk. *(J.A. at 1016.)*

II.

Based upon the foregoing statements, Wells filed a defamation suit in the United States District Court for the District of Maryland on April 1, 1997.[10] Wells asserted that Liddy defamed her

---

9. The parties did not provide a URL for this site.

10. The face of Wells's complaint indicates some confusion over the basis for federal court jurisdiction over this suit. Although the complaint cites 28 U.S.C.A. § 1331 (West 1993), the statute governing federal question jurisdiction, the complaint recites the grounds for diversity jurisdiction under 28 U.S.C.A. § 1332 (West 1993 & Supp. 1999). Because complete diversity is present and defamation is a state law matter, we construe this as a diversity suit.

by stating to public audiences on several occasions that she acted as a procurer of prostitutes for men who visited the DNC. Particularly, Wells asserted that Liddy defamed her during the JMU speech, during the cruise ship speech, on the *Don and Mike Show,* and in the Accuracy in Media web site.[11] The complaint sought one million dollars in damages for injury to reputation, one million dollars in damages for mental suffering and three million dollars in punitive damages. Liddy filed his Answer on April 28, 1997, and the case proceeded to discovery....

---

11. Wells also initially claimed that Liddy had defamed her on his radio show and during a broadcast of the television show *Hardball. See* Hardball *(CNBC television broadcast, June 16, 1997).* Wells voluntarily dismissed these claims, however, prior to the district court's summary judgment ruling.

In the Wells trial, the floor plan of the sixth-floor headquarters of the Democratic National Committee in the Watergate office building was used as evidence that the real target of the second Watergate break-in was the desk belonging to secretary Ida "Maxie" Wells. The area marked with an "X" is where the police entered. The area marked with a circle is where the burglars were apprehended, near Wells's desk. Directly across the street from the terrace (top of floor plan) was the seventh-floor Howard Johnson's hotel room used to monitor Wells's telephone. The two big offices in the lower corners housed the DNC chairman, Lawrence O'Brien, and the treasurer, Robert Strauss. Neither office could be seen from the Howard Johnson's surveillance room; moreover, our surveillance post could not have monitored these offices using the type of listening device ("bug") that was discovered, or the type we were actually using, which was much more sophisticated. *(1 page)*

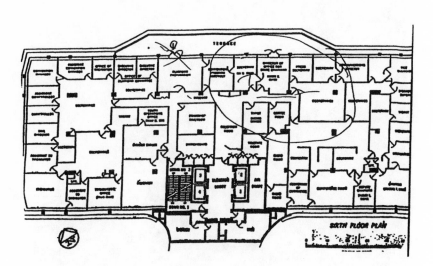

This police photograph shows the evidence seized at the crime scene from the Watergate burglars. Note the key taped to a notebook (foreground); burglar Eugenio Martinez, who was using the operational alias Jean Valdes, repeatedly risked his life to conceal this key. *(1 page)*

These handwritten police notes reveal the results of the search of the burglars' persons. Note that Eugenio Martinez, under the alias Jean Valdes, was found to possess "1 yellow spiral note book w/Key taped to front." *(1 page)*

The notebook that police took from Eugenio Martinez; the taped key has been removed and photographed with it. *(1 page)*

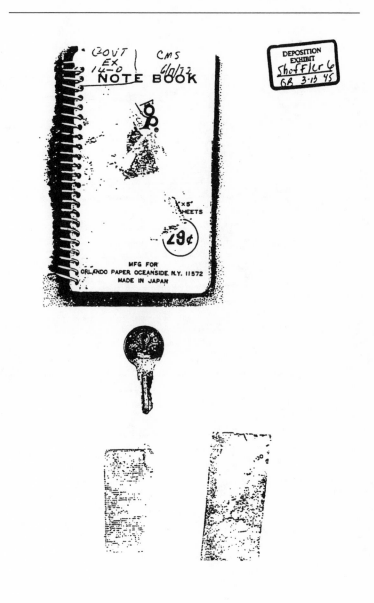

This FBI report, dated 27 June 1972, reveals that the key taken from burglar Eugenio Martinez fit but one lock in DNC headquarters—the lock on Ida "Maxie" Wells's desk. It is, literally, the key to Watergate. *(1 page)*

FEDERAL BUREAU OF INVESTIGATION

1

CONFIDENTIAL   Date of transcription   6/27/72

    Mrs. MARIE CUNINGHAM, Secretary, Democratic National Committee (DNC), 2600 Virginia Avenue, N.W., was accompanied by SA KING, while she tried various locks, at DNC, with a vanguard key number ML-311.

    After trying numerous locks, it was determined that key ML-311, fit the desk of MAXIE WELLS.

On 6/27/72 at Washington, D.C. File # WFO 139-166

SAS MICHAEL J. KING
AND DONALD E. STREET MJK:vjm   Date dictated 6/27/72

The 9 June 1972 newspaper article that precipitated the second, famous Watergate break-in. This front-page story revealed that the FBI had uncovered a call-girl ring being run out of the Columbia Plaza Apartments (which are in close proximity to the Watergate) and that the lawyer for the call-girl ring had been indicted. That day, 9 June,

Jeb Magruder, de facto deputy to John Mitchell at the Committee to Reelect the President (CRP), asked me whether I could make a second, unscheduled entry into the Watergate. I told him I could, and received orders to do so on Monday, 12 June. *(2 pages)*

INDICTMENT
Call-Girl Operation Uncovered

Continued From Page A-1

then induced them to pose for "personal" photographs — some of them nude — which Bailley allegedly said would be for his personal use, according to the sources.

Sometime. after the photographs were taken, the sources said, Bailley would use them to blackmail the girls — threatening to send copies to the girls' employers if they did not engage in prostitution.

According to the indictment, Bailley began his operation in November 1969 and continued until Feb. 16, 1972.

The sources said the White House secretary was not one of the women listed in today's indictment because her case did not involve crossing state lines.

White House Client

The sources stressed that no high officials either on Capitol Hill or at the White House were involved in running the ring, but they did indicate that a White House lawyer was a client.

It was learned that a subpoena several weeks ago of a White House employe prompted a phone call from White House aide Peter Flanigan to the U.S. Attorney's Office.

No one in the office would acknowledge that such a phone call was made. But sources outside the office said Flanigan apparently called to find out if there was any chance of embarrassment to the Nixon administration.

Numerous counts of the indictment accuse Bailley of communicating "threats to injure the reputation" of the women involved.

Bailley, a graduate of Catholic University's law school, was vehement in denials after being informed of the indictment.

"It's untrue, absolutely untrue," he said. "I was positive they wouldn't indict me. They've done i n c r e d i b l e things. You're talking to a wrecked man."

Bailley, who said he had spent five years in a seminary in Baltimore, said he had known that a special grand jury was sitting.

"They've called dozens of people — women who are upper-class people, college graduates," he said.

Bailley said he had defended "small-time pimps in Washington in routine prostitution cases" in his private law practice, and indicated that he thought some of them were trying to get back at him.

"I'll sue the government," he said.

"I am absolutely innocent. My telephone has been tapped. People have been told not to talk to me. I've worked for everything I've ever gotten. I am not a pimp."

Denies All Charges

Bailley repeatedly denied the charges in a conversation, at one point saying, "I swear to God it's untrue."

He said he had not talked to the women who, he said, originated the complaint. "One night she called me up but the telephone was tapped," he said.

He said he had abandoned his law office about two months ago "after the FBI s e a r c h e d it — they've searched my home, they've followed me to Florida, to California. At Rehoboth Beach, I took some pictures of some people on the beach and the FBI questioned them."

He added that "the FBI has told people not to talk to me."

Of his version of the story, Bailley said "there are at least 15 people who can verify it I just can't believe it."

He said that "all I have is a '68 Camaro — I haven't got any money. I worked my way through high school and college and law school I've worked for everything I've ever gotten."

Bailley said he is a native of Upper Marlboro and is divorced.

According to a list recently compiled, Bailley was paid $20,708.25 in Criminal Justice Act funds for defending indigents in 1971.

This Secret Service Appointment Record proves that at 3:50 P.M. on Friday, 9 June 1972, John Rudy—the assistant United States attorney responsible for investigating and prosecuting the lawyer for the Columbia Plaza call-girl ring—reported as ordered to John Dean at the White House. This was the *very same day* that newspapers carried the story of the indictment of the call-girl ring's lawyer. *(1 page)*

The letter Ida Wells wrote to her friend Joann in which she said, "They've [the Republicans] got the makings for a good scandal in my case...." *(2 pages)*

1

Sunday night

I haven't gotten around to mailing this yet, it's just as well because I've developed a crisis since then. I was subpoenaed (sp?) on Saturday to appear before the Grand Jury in Washington on Wednesday. I'm flying up tomorrow to talk to Spencer & the DNC lawyers plus to get one of my own maybe. It appears that the Republicans are going to try to discredit Demo. witnesses on moral grounds. They've got the makings for a good scandal in my case because I lived with those guys Joe etc. — and they apparently know a lot of it. Spencer & I both feel (hope really) that I probably won't be important enough for them to bother, but I am really upset & nervous & will really be glad when it's all over. The FBI has a file on me a mile long now, which isn't any big deal, & I may have to bare [or ?] [...] in court, which also isn't

so terrible — but I am really afraid
the press will take off + run with
all of this when they smell gossip
the other records will be private,
+ I don't think I've broken any
laws, but you can understand
my nerves. I doubt seriously
if anyone at the house will mention the Ngate incident to me,
but please squelch any discussion
of it at all + say things are fine
Also better get rid of this; I
shouldn't write, but must confide
in someone.
    I'm enclosing a pg. from the
Inc Beacon which you might not
ave seen. Infamy in all places.
    I will write Jim, Bill, Gordy, +
Ian my thanks for their parts in
my vacation, but prefer to wait
until I'm thinking better. Meanwhile, please express thanks for
me + tell them they'll hear
from me.
    Thanks again for a wonderful
vacation. It's a good thing I
got my head straight + my body re-
...while I could. If you talk to...

In 1999, the United States Court of Appeals for the Fourth Circuit ruled that there was sufficient evidence in the Wells case to warrant a jury trial. After a long trial in the United States District Court in Baltimore, the jury, on 1 February 2001, hung, split 7 to 2 in my favor, and Judge Motz granted judgment for me as a matter of law on the grounds that no "reasonable jury" could have found that I "had been negligent in making the allegedly defamatory remarks upon which Wells's suit was based."

The *Washington Post,* its huge investment in the bogus Woodward and Bernstein theory of Watergate torpedoed below the waterline and in a terminal list to port, erupted in editorial fury on 4 February 2001:

> Courts are a capricious venue for arguments about history. Sometimes, as when a British court last year resoundingly rejected the Holocaust denial of "historian" David Irving, litigation can help protect established history from those who would maliciously rewrite it. But conspiracy theorizing generally is better addressed in the public arena by rigorous confrontation with facts. That's true both out of respect for freedom of speech—even wrong-headed speech—and because historical truth does not always fare so well in court. A jury in Tennessee in 1999 embraced the looniest of conspiracy theories concerning the assassination of Martin Luther King Jr. And this week, in a federal court in Baltimore, the commonly understood and well-founded history of the Watergate scandal took a hit as well.

The forum was the defamation case of G. Gordon Liddy, the Watergate felon and radio talk-show host, who has promoted in speeches a "revisionist"—false would be a better description—account of the scandal. Mr. Liddy has argued that the burglary was not an attempt to collect political intelligence on President Nixon's enemies but an effort masterminded by then-White House counsel John Dean to steal pictures of prostitutes—including Mr. Dean's then-girlfriend and current wife—from the desk of a secretary at the Democratic headquarters. The secretary, Ida Wells, is now a community college teacher in Louisiana and was understandably offended by the implication that she was somehow involved in a call girl ring. She sued Mr. Liddy, and the battle has dragged on for four years.

The jury failed to reach a unanimous verdict, but it split overwhelmingly in favor of Mr. Liddy; the majority of jurors felt that Ms. Wells's lawyers had failed to prove his theory wrong. They found this in spite of the fact that Mr. Liddy relies, for his theory, on a disbarred attorney with a history of mental illness. The call girl theory "is possible," one juror told Post staff writer Manuel Roig-Franzia. "It sure makes me more curious." "We'll never know" what happened, said another.

The danger of such outcomes as this one is that this sort of thinking spreads. For whether or not Mr. Liddy's comments legally defamed Ms. Wells, we do know what happened at Watergate—and it had nothing to do with prostitutes.

In his published decision, dated 19 March 2001, Judge Motz ripped the *Post* a new one (though the judge referred to it simply as "a respected newspaper"), while teaching it a much-needed lesson on the First Amendment:

Chief Judge J. Frederick Motz's decision in the Wells case. On page 11 of the decision, Judge Motz chastised the *Washington Post* for its overheated editorial regarding the court's decision. *(12 pages)*

IN THE UNITED STATES DISTRICT COURT
FOR THE DISTRICT OF MARYLAND

IDA MAXWELL WELLS   *

v.   *   Civil No. JFM-97-946

G. GORDON LIDDY   *

•••••

MEMORANDUM

On February 1, 2001, I issued an oral opinion granting defendant's motion for judgment as a matter of law after the jury had announced it would be unable to render a verdict. Applying the standard set forth by Fed. R. Civ. P. 50(a),[2] I found that no "reasonable jury" could have found in favor of plaintiff Ida Maxwell Wells against defendant G. Gordon Liddy on the issue of whether Liddy had been negligent in making the allegedly defamatory remarks upon which Wells's suit was based.[2] On February 6, 2001, I entered an order implementing my oral opinion. In that order I indicated I might enter a supplemental written opinion in the event of an appeal.

---

[1]In making this determination, I have viewed the evidence in the light most favorable to Wells, the non-moving party, and given her the benefit of all reasonable inferences. See Herold v. Hajoca Corp., 864 F.2d 317, 319 (4th Cir. 1988) (citations omitted).

[2]With the consent of counsel, I submitted a special verdict form to the jury permitting it to select one of two questions to answer first: whether Wells had proved the falsity of the allegedly defamatory statements or whether she had proved that Liddy had acted negligently in making them. A unanimous "no" answer to either of the questions would have made consideration of the other question unnecessary. In a post-trial interview with counsel and me, the jurors indicated they were split seven to two in favor of Liddy on both questions. Several of the jurors confirmed this vote in a separate interview or interviews newspaper reporters conducted of them.
I granted Liddy's motion for judgment as a matter of law solely on the negligence issue. On the truth/falsity issue, Wells's testimony denying that there were any pictures of prostitutes in her desk that were shown to visitors to the DNC headquarters is itself sufficient to create a jury question.

This memorandum constitutes that opinion. My discussion assumes a reader is knowledgeable about the facts and issues as set forth in the earlier published opinions in the case. See Wells v. Liddy, 186 F.3d 505 (4th Cir. 1999), rev'g 1 F. Supp. 2d 532 (D. Md. 1998).

I.

In its opinion on the prior appeal in this case, the Fourth Circuit held I erred in finding that Liddy was entitled to summary judgment on Wells's claims for presumed and punitive damages. The Fourth Circuit disagreed with my conclusion that the record established that Wells would be unable to prove that Liddy acted with actual malice in making alleged defamatory statements about her on two occasions: once during a question and answer session after a motivational speech he made at James Madison University and again during a talk he gave while on a cruise ship. 186 F.3d at 544. I recognize that my granting of Liddy's motion for judgment as a matter of law might be seen to be at odds with the Fourth Circuit's ruling since I am finding that Wells's evidence fails to meet the lower standard of negligence the parties agree (in light of the Fourth Circuit's further holding that Wells is not an involuntary public figure) applies to her compensatory damage claim.[3] However, I am now ruling after the establishment of a trial record that is fuller and more clarifying than was the record on summary judgment.

The question posed by Liddy's motion for judgment is whether Wells presented sufficient evidence from which a reasonable jury could find that Liddy failed to take reasonable steps in assessing the truth of his allegedly false statements. According to the Fourth Circuit, the portion

---

[3]As I indicated in my oral opinion after trial, I continue to believe that Wells is an involuntary public figure. However, both in instructing the jury and in considering the sufficiency of the evidence, I have, of course, applied a negligence standard.

of Liddy's remarks on which the case turns is his statement that there were pictures of prostitutes in Wells's desk that were shown to visitors to the DNC headquarters interested in call girl services. The sole source of this information was Phillip Bailley. The question thus becomes whether Liddy reasonably assessed the veracity of what Bailley told him about the pictures allegedly in Wells's desk.

Bailley has a history of mental illness, and his personal involvement in prostitution activities around the time of the Watergate break-ins led to a felony conviction and his disbarment as a lawyer. Liddy was aware there were doubts about Bailley's credibility, and Liddy's own counsel had advised him not to rely exclusively upon Bailley. Thus, to borrow a phrase frequently used in instructions concerning the believability of felons, cooperators, accomplices, and the like in criminal cases. Liddy was required to examine Bailley's statements with caution and weigh them with great care. Liddy was not, however, required to discard those statements entirely, and for the following reasons I find that Wells failed to produce sufficient evidence at trial from which a jury could reasonably find that he acted negligently in giving credit to them.

I note at the outset that although the fact is certainly not dispositive, the evidence reveals that Liddy did not obtain the information from Bailley in a casual conversation. He spoke with Bailley in the presence of one Susan Fenley, a third party whose presence was requested by Bailley. At one point, according to notes that Liddy transcribed immediately after the interview, Fenley interrupted Bailley to say: "You are getting into very heavy stuff, now. Are you on the record?" According to Liddy's notes. Bailley continued on, without paying heed to what Fenley had said.

The record is also clear that Liddy did not simply rely upon his own assessment of Bailley's credibility. A call girl theory of Watergate had emerged in the literature in 1984 when James Hougan had authored a book entitled Secret Agenda. In 1991, the same year in which Liddy conducted his interview of Bailley, another book, Silent Coup, written by Leonard Colodny, expanded upon the theory. From conversations with Hougan and Colodny, Liddy was aware that Bailley had given them essentially the same information that Bailley gave him about the contents of Wells's desk. Colodny did not testify at trial. Hougan, however, did appear as a witness, and his testimony dispelled any inference that he is a fanatical conspiracy theorist whose name Liddy simply has invoked to provide cover for his crediting of Bailley.[4] A former Washington editor for Harper's, Hougan brought to his study of Watergate a perspective far different from Liddy's. Further, as Liddy knew, Hougan's work had received favorable reviews from his peers, including J. Anthony Lukas, a Pulitzer Prize winning author. Thus, the record establishes that Liddy, in making his own assessment of Bailley's credibility, could responsibly rely upon Hougan's judgment that Bailley was telling the truth, just as any professional may rely upon the clinical judgment of another.

The record also establishes that Liddy tested what Bailley told him by independent investigation. He studied relevant literature and conducted interviews of his own. Before

---

[4]By suggesting that Hougan made a favorable impression at trial, I do not intend to invade the province of the fact-finders. Of course, it was entirely up to the jury to determine whether Hougan was telling the truth about the matters to which he testified. However, the appearance Hougan projects is itself a relevant fact in determining whether Liddy could reasonably rely upon him, and to the extent that the cold record does not adequately portray that appearance, I am simply adding my own observation. In any event, the point is not critical to my decision.

making the statements upon which Wells's claims are based, he also had the benefit of numerous

depositions taken in an earlier defamation suit John and Maureen Dean had filed against him. St.

Martin's Press, and others in the District of Columbia.[5] The materials available to Liddy

reflected various facts that he could reasonably consider to be corroborative of what Bailley had

said.[6]

First, Liddy knew that the evidence is overwhelming that Eugenio Martinez, one of the

Watergate burglars, had a desk key in his possession (taped to a spiral notebook) on the night of

the second break-in. Liddy also knew the evidence is undisputed that the only lock at the DNC

headquarters that the key fit was the lock to Wells's desk. In its prior opinion the Fourth Circuit

indicated that this fact corroborated only the call girl theory in general, not what Bailley

specifically said about the contents of Wells's desk. However, at that time the Fourth Circuit did

not have the benefit of a complete trial record. While the placing of a tap on Spencer Oliver's

telephone line that was accessible through an extension on Wells's desk may only support the

call girl theory generally, the fact that one of the burglars had a key to the desk specifically ties

---

[5]This case had its origins in the <u>Dean</u> litigation. Wells's present counsel, who was then representing the Deans (but not her), attended the James Madison University event where Liddy was speaking and tape-recorded the allegedly defamatory remarks. He then transcribed those remarks and, apparently believing that it was in the Deans's interest to have parallel litigation instituted against Liddy, had a copy of the transcript sent to Wells and encouraged her to sue.

The <u>Dean</u> suit has been concluded by an out-of-court resolution. However, as Liddy's trial testimony made clear, the acrimony between the Deans and himself remains. Therefore, since the Deans are not parties to the present case and since the aspects of Liddy's call girl theory implicating John Dean in the second Watergate break-in are tawdry and unnecessary to the resolution of the issues now presented, I will refrain from discussing them.

[6]It is worth noting that there was evidence that Bailley made uncorroborated accusations implicating other persons in the call girl ring that Liddy did not repeat.

the desk to that theory. Wells presented no evidence at trial concerning anything else she kept in her desk in which the Watergate burglars might have been interested, and she has suggested no alternative explanation as to why Martinez possessed the key.

Second, Liddy knew that Carl Shoffler, the same arresting officer who seized the key from Martinez, had testified on deposition in the Dean case that a camera placed by the burglars was found on Wells's desk.[7] This testimony tends to reflect that something of interest to the burglars was in or around Wells's desk.

Third, Liddy knew from various sources, including the deposition of Alfred Baldwin taken in the Dean case, that conversations of a sexual nature had been intercepted over Oliver's tapped telephone line.[8] While not specifically supporting Bailley's assertion that pictures of prostitutes were kept in Wells's desk, these conversations provide part of the context in which the credibility of that assertion must be judged.

Fourth, Liddy was aware that the conventional theory of the reason for the Watergate break-ins - to obtain political intelligence from a tap on the telephone of Larry O'Brien, the chairman of the DNC - has long been subject to question. The bugging equipment alleged to have been used required a line of sight between the tap and the interceptor; no line of sight existed between O'Brien's telephone and the Howard Johnson hotel room across the street from the DNC headquarters where the interceptor was located. Likewise, no tap was ever found on O'Brien's phone. Further, several experienced observers (including Charles Colson, who

---

[7]Shoffler is deceased, and his testimony at trial was presented by videotape deposition.

[8]Baldwin was the person who listened to, and kept a log of, the illegally intercepted conversations.

testified by videotape deposition at trial) have questioned the view that savvy political operatives would have expected to learn sensitive political information, as opposed to organizational and financial information, from a tap on telephones at the national headquarters of a major political party.

Fifth, Liddy knew of deposition testimony from the <u>Dean</u> case by Jack Rudy, who was the Assistant United States Attorney in charge of the grand jury investigation of prostitution resulting in Bailley's indictment. Rudy had testified that one of his informants, the alleged madam of a call girl ring being run at the Columbia Plaza apartment complex near the Watergate, "mentioned Spencer Oliver [to Rudy] in the sense that [Oliver] knew of or had been involved in some way in the Columbia Plaza operation." Moreover, according to Rudy, "one of the FBI agents identified one of the coded names [in an address book seized from Bailley] as being a person who worked either at or with the DNC." When asked what that person did at or with the DNC, Rudy answered, "I'm stretching to say that she was a secretary or administrative aide of some type. Administrative aide is what I want to say, but I don't believe she came up to doing that. That would imply she was a higher person. I think she was more of a - like an executive secretary or something." Further, Rudy testified, "[i]t seems to me that . . . this was a female who arranged for liaisons. It was kind of a go-between." Of course, this testimony constituted hearsay, and it was not admissible on the truth/falsity issue. However, it was admissible concerning Liddy's state of mind and provided corroboration for what he had been told by Bailley.

Sixth, Wells testified she cannot recall having known Bailley. However, Liddy knew that Bailley's sister, Jeanine Bailley Ball, testified on deposition in the <u>Dean</u> case (as she did at trial) that while she was a teenager, she worked as a secretary in her brother's law office and that a woman identifying herself as Maxie Wells called in on numerous occasions asking to speak to Phillip Bailley. Wells attacks Ball's credibility on this point. Perhaps her attack is well founded, perhaps it is not. However, nothing in the record demonstrates that Ball is so inherently unreliable that Liddy was unreasonable in crediting what she said. Her testimony provided a basis for him to conclude that Wells has not been forthcoming about her relationship with Bailley.

Seventh, Officer Shoffler was present on the day shortly after the second break-in when Wells learned that a piece of photographic equipment had been found on her desk. According to his deposition testimony in the Dean case, Wells "made a surprise sort of - I characterize it as a shocked look and [said] something to the effect of, 'My God, they haven't gone in there,' or something to that effect." Further, Shoffler recalled that the person standing behind Wells (whom he later was led to believe was Spencer Oliver) "was more calm" and "was very emphatic in terms of how he looked at her, [saying] 'Well, there's nothing in there of any importance anyway.'"

Eighth, Wells produced in discovery in this case a letter she wrote (but never sent) to one of her close friends immediately after it was publicly disclosed that Oliver's phone had been tapped.[9] Liddy learned of the letter after he had made his speech at James Madison University but before making his remarks on the cruise ship. Thus, it is relevant to his state of mind when he

---

[9]According to a proffer made by defense counsel, this letter was contained in a box of Watergate-related materials turned over by Wells that, when deposed, Wells stated she had not looked into for twenty-five years.

made the second of his allegedly defamatory statements. Wells began her letter by referring to

another note she was enclosing:

> I haven't gotten around to mailing this yet; it's just as well because I've
> developed a crisis since then. I was subpoenoed (sp?) on Saturday to appear
> before the Grand Jury in Washington on Wednesday. I'm flying up tomorrow to
> talk to Spencer & the DNC lawyers, plus to get one of my own maybe.

She continued:

> It appears that the Republicans are going to try to discredit Demo. witnesses on
> moral grounds. They've got the makings for a good scandal in my case because
> I've lived with those guys, Joe, etc. - and they apparently know a lot of it.
> Spencer & I both feel (hope, really) that I probably won't be important enough for
> them to bother, but I am really upset & nervous & will really be glad when it's all
> over. The FBI has a file on me a mile long now, which isn't any big deal, & I
> may have to bare (or bear) all in court, which also isn't so terrible - but I am really
> afraid the press will take off & run with all of this when they smell gossip. The
> other records will be private, & I don't think I've broken any laws, but you can
> understand my nerves.

She added, "I doubt seriously if anyone at the house will mention the W'gate incident to me, but

please squelch any discussion of it at all & say things are fine. Also better get rid of this; I

shouldn't write, but must confide in someone." Wells closed the letter by referring to herself as a

friend "who needs help keeping her nose clean."

On deposition and at trial Wells testified that all she was alluding to in this letter was the

fact that she lived in a house with five male acquaintances (in a room off by itself) and that she

had been involved in conversations over the tapped telephone line during which she gossiped

about the personal lives of other persons at the DNC. Nothing in the letter necessarily contradicts

this explanation. However, a reasonable person would not necessarily find the explanation

satisfactory, and might conclude instead that the letter reflected that Wells had been engaged in

questionable activities.

9

In sum, the record is replete with facts that Liddy could reasonably believe support Bailley's statements about the contents of Wells's desk. This is not to say, of course, that what Bailley said was true or that the call girl theory is accurate. That is not the question. The dispositive point is that Wells had the burden of proving that Liddy lacked a reasonable basis for expressing the allegedly defamatory remarks about her, and the evidence was insufficient to sustain that burden.

II.

One can certainly sympathize with Wells's plight of being caught up in the resurrection of events that occurred decades ago and over which she may never have possessed control. However, for the reasons I have stated, she has not met her burden of proof on the negligence issue. Moreover, her claims raise serious First Amendment concerns. Her avowed purpose in pursuing the litigation (as expressed during her trial testimony) is to prevent any further public discussion about facts connecting her desk and the telephone on the desk to the motives of the Watergate burglars.

The conventional "political intelligence" theory of the Watergate break-ins, first articulated by the majority report of the Senate Select Committee investigating the Watergate affair, may be correct. The call girl theory. or some part of it, may be correct instead. Alternatively, there may be truth in neither theory, or in both. Different participants and their principals may have had different motives. some to obtain political intelligence, others to garner information with which to embarrass or compromise their political opponents. But whatever the truth may be, one thing should be certain: free debate about important public issues must be tolerated, provided that the debate (when it potentially damages the reputations of private persons)

10

does not exceed the bounds of reason.

In the wake of the mistrial in this case,[10] an editorial in a respected newspaper opined, "Courts are a capricious venue for arguments about history. . . . [C]onspiracy theorizing generally is better addressed in the public arena by rigorous confrontation with facts." These observations certainly may be true. But the editorial did not stop there. Decrying the views of the jurors who were prepared to find in favor of Liddy and their conclusion that Wells had failed to prove his theory wrong, the editorial went on to say:

> The call girl theory "is possible," one juror . . . [said]. "It sure makes me curious." "We'll never know" what happened, said another. The danger of such outcomes as this one is that this sort of thinking spreads. For whether or not Mr. Liddy's comments legally defamed Ms. Wells, we do know what happened at Watergate - and it had nothing to do with prostitutes.

Apparently, in the editorialist's view, the book on Watergate has been forever closed. But spreading "this sort of thinking" - fresh, inquisitive, and demanding of proof - is precisely what the First Amendment is all about. Individually and as a people, in order to prevent our minds from narrowing, we must be wary of ourselves, subjecting our own premises, spoken or unspoken, to critical self-scrutiny. We must be equally skeptical about pronouncements of allegedly unalterable truths asserted by those who proclaim exclusive knowledge. We must remain open to reasonable discussion, challenging our own ideas and those of others. No one familiar with the record in this case would pretend that it has brought finality to what assuredly will be a continuing debate about the reasons for the Watergate break-ins. As the jurors criticized

---

[10]As noted in footnote 2, supra, seven of the nine persons representing the common sense of the community, after hearing all of the evidence, did not find Liddy's statements to have been proven false. That fact alone highlights the constitutional cost of subjecting Liddy to the time and expense of a second trial.

in the editorial recognized, the trial raised far more questions than it answered. It is the pursuit of those questions, however, that the First Amendment protects. To make that protection real, this litigation must come to an end.

Date: March 19, 2001

J. Frederick Motz
United States District Judge

Miss Wells appealed Judge Motz's decision to the United States Court of Appeals for the Fourth Circuit, which, in its decision of 1 March 2002, stated, *inter alia:*

> We conclude that the evidence enumerated by the district court does not support judgment as a matter of law because it fails to prove, as a matter of law, that Liddy's actions were prudent. In other words, the question of whether Liddy was negligent presents a genuine issue of material fact for a jury to resolve and, therefore, the district court erred in granting judgment as a matter of law in Liddy's favor. Consequently, we reverse the district court's judgment and remand for a new trial.

That new trial was held between 21 June and 3 July 2002 in the United States District Court in Baltimore. By this time, Judge Motz had retired as chief judge and been replaced by the Honorable Frederic N. Smalkin.

At the trial, I introduced dramatic new evidence that the electronic listening device ("bug") supposedly "found" by the Democrats in 1972 had been introduced into evidence by the assistant United States attorneys prosecuting my 1973 trial in spite of the fact that the FBI laboratory had told them it was a phony and, obviously, a "plant." I produced the following memorandum, dated 2 October 1972, from W. W. Bradley, believed to be the chief of the FBI laboratory's electronics section, to the assistant director of the FBI in charge of the laboratory, in which Bradley forcefully refuted the chief assistant U.S. attorney's claims about the listening device:

The assistant United States attorneys prosecuting my 1973
trial produced an electronic listening device ("bug") that they claimed the
Watergate burglars had placed to monitor conversations. In this memorandum, however, the FBI laboratory showed how the device could not have

---

UNITED STATES GOVERNMENT

Memorandum

    M. A. Conrad   DATE: 10/2/72

'OM :   W. W. Bradley

                                   1 - Mr. Felt

suject: JAMES WALTER MC CORD, JR.; ET AL.   1 - Mr. Bates
        BURGLARY OF DEMOCRATIC PARTY   1 - Mr. Bolz
        NATIONAL HEADQUARTERS, 6/17/72   1 - Mr. Conrad
        INTERCEPTION OF COMMUNICATIONS   1 - Mr. Bradley
                                         1 - Mr. Miller

        Memorandum of 9/29/72 from Mr. Bolz to Mr. Bates relative to the
above-entitled matter attaches a memorandum from Assistant U. S. Attorney
(AUSA) Earl Silbert to Assistant Attorney General Henry E. Peterson dated
9/28/72. AUSA Silbert in his memorandum deals with the electronic device
recovered from the telephone of Spencer Oliver on 9/13/72 and sets forth his
belief that the recovered device is the original device which permitted Baldwin to
overhear conversations. Silbert sets forth five reasons which he believes lead
to his conclusion. Laboratory is requested to review and reply.

        Review shows that none of the reasons are conclusive or compelling
and that only the first reason advanced by Silbert is technical in nature and based
reported technical facts. The remaining four reasons are questionable or
speculative in nature, and in at least one instance (#5) totally in error. The
specific reasons cited by Silbert and Laboratory comments relative to each one set
out below using Silbert's numbering.

        1. SILBERT: The device recovered opera 1 at 120 MHz. Baldwin
was receiving at 118.9 MHz, well within the range of the device. The three devices
in the possession of those arrested operated two at 110, one at 114 MHz, not at all
as clearly within the range of the receiver at 118.9, particularly the one operating
at 110.

        LABORATORY COMMENT: The frequency on which the recovered
device originally may have operated, if at all, cannot be accurately determined
since it was inoperative at time of recovery. It was made operable by replacing
a defective transistor, after which the unit operated on 120 MHz. While this
is closest of the four mentioned devices, this fact is not conclusive because

RAM:lt
(7)

                CONTINUED - OVER

ALL INFORMATION CONTAINED
HEREIN IS UNCLASSIFIED
DATE 5/2/95 BY

9 NOV 1 6 1972

been one received and monitored by my lookout, Mr. Baldwin, in the Howard Johnson's across the street because (a) it was inoperable and (b) when made operable, it was on the wrong frequency. It was also totally unlike any of the listening devices with which my men were equipped when captured. *(4 pages)*

Memorandum to Mr. Conrad
RE: JAMES WALTER MC CORD, JR.; ET AL
BURGLARY OF DEMOCRATIC PARTY
NATIONAL HEADQUARTERS, 6/17/72
INTERCEPTION OF COMMUNICATIONS

(a) there is no evidence to our knowledge that limits the original device tuned in by Baldwin to one of the four recovered (It is our understanding that two men escaped from the premises the night of discovery) (b) the original operating frequency of instant device cannot be determined; and (c) after repair, the operating frequency is not on the frequency reportedly received.

2. SILBERT: To assume that one of the three devices recovered upon arrest was the one used on Oliver's telephone assumes that the defendants removed it. I see no reason to assume that. A more or at least equally logical assumption is that they were going to put more taps on, not take those they had in out. Clearly, they were going to put the bugging device in. Why not the taps?

While the Oliver tap was not O'Brien, they apparently had considered it to be producing useful information. There was, accordingly, no reason to remove it while putting in other taps.

LABORATORY COMMENT: Reason appears speculative. We do not know the basis validating the assumption "Clearly, they were going to put the bugging device in." Laboratory tests of the batteries associated with the bugging device showed that some were partially run down. This would not be the normally expected condition for a new installation of batteries. However, more in point, the absence of a device in Oliver's phone at the time of the security check does not necessarily carry with it the assumption that one of the devices found in possession of defendants was the one heard by Baldwin.

3. SILBERT: The location of the tap in the telephone is totally consistent with Baldwin's explanation of how the telephone calls were intercepted – only three specific extensions, one at a time.

LABORATORY COMMENT: Questionable reason. Summary Bureau report dated 9/20/72 made available to Laboratory states on page 12 that Baldwin in his monitoring discovered that he could overhear telephone conversation on four extensions of one phone at the office of Oliver. General Investigative Division advises that Baldwin's interviews tend to indicate he believed he was monitoring conversations of secretaries and others from telephones which were extensions of Oliver's phone. The instant device, as installed at time of recovery would not permit this type of operation.

- 2 -

Memorandum to Mr. Conrad
RE: JAMES WALTER MC CORD, JR.; ET AL.
BURGLARY OF DEMOCRATIC PARTY
NATIONAL HEADQUARTERS, 6/17/72
INTERCEPTION OF COMMUNICATIONS

4. SILBERT: I cannot imagine anyone planting a device in the Democratic headquarters after Watergate, particularly on Oliver's telephone. It is too ludicrous.

LABORATORY COMMENT: Speculative reason. At least two other possibilities suggest themselves on the basis of reported information:

(a) Bureau Summary report dated 9/20/72 shows on page 11 that some intercepted conversations dealt with marital problems. Marital problems are a well recognized basis for attempted wiretapping.

(b) Democrats or sympathizers, feeling they had unusually good issue in the "burglary" and wiretapping incident, could have decided to make a more recent "installation" and call attention to it in order to keep the pot boiling. Baldwin had previously disclosed approximate frequency and fact Oliver's phone was involved. WFO wire dated 9/15/72 sets out that Oliver's office cognizant of at least part of this information. Moreover, O'Brien has recently publicly alleged his office was bugged.

In this regard it is of possible significance that the device found on Oliver's phone on 9/13/72 was completely unlike the devices found in possession of defendants at time of arrest.

5. SILBERT: I think the FBI missed it because the location of Oliver's office in the Democratic headquarters is such that it is almost the last place one would expect a tap to be placed – nowhere near O'Brien's office or anywhere else of importance.

LABORATORY COMMENT: Totally erroneous reason. Laboratory's search was not keyed to relative location. Indeed, Laboratory technical personnel, in addition to knowing of attempted penetration by arrested defendants, also considered possibility Democrat sympathizers might make additional installations to exacerbate the situation, and therefore all rooms and all phones were considered highly suspect and were thoroughly searched.

*By false trouble report. In this regard WFO wire 9/30/72, advises telephone repairman attempted to observe malfunctions reported by secretary with negative results. WFO suggests possibility reported malfunction had never occurred.

- 3 -

Memorandum to Mr. Conrad
RE: JAMES WALTER MC CORD, JR.; ET AL
BURGLARY OF DEMOCRATIC PARTY
NATIONAL HEADQUARTERS, 6/17/72
INTERCEPTION OF COMMUNICATIONS

SUMMARY: While we recognize the appeal, from a prosecution standpoint, of the situation postulated by AUSA Silbert, no facts known to us at present support the presence of a listening device on Oliver's telephone at the time of the security check. There is no evidence to our knowledge that the device heard by Baldwin was heard by anyone after the arrest of the defendants. On the contrary, a check of the telephones by competent and experienced technical personnel, looking specifically for this type of device, showed no such device to be present at the time of the search. In this regard, Supervisor W. G. Stevens who was in personal charge of and took part in the search has previously stated that the device was large enough to be readily seen by physical search, and that based on the search conducted, he is positive that the device was not on the phone at the time of the search. Further in this regard, it is noted that the physical security of the Democratic National Committee space was such as to make subsequent access for the purpose of installing devices relatively easy. WFO wire to the Bureau dated 9/15/72 on page 6 states DNCH maintained no limitation to access to offices after normal duty hours until about midnight when premises secured.

ACTION:

If approved a response to Assistant Attorney General Peterson will be prepared along the above lines.

- 4 -

On the day the case went to the jury, 3 July 2002, Gail Gibson of the *Baltimore Sun* wrote in part:

> The federal judge presiding over a $5 million defamation case against G. Gordon Liddy said yesterday that the Watergate figure had built a strong circumstantial case to back his claims that the infamous burglary was tied to a call-girl ring.
>
> Chief U.S. District Judge Frederic N. Smalkin refused for a second time to dismiss the case being heard in Baltimore. But he said Liddy's accuser had presented little evidence to show that Liddy was reckless in promoting his alternate theory of Watergate without admissions from key figures.
>
> "I would suggest... that very few people at the Democratic National Committee would be willing to talk about a nest of whores if they were involved in the DNC in the 1970s," Smalkin said, noting that Liddy's reliance on circumstantial evidence wasn't a surprise. "How else is he going to get corroborating evidence?" ...

On 3 July 2002, Judge Smalkin gave the case to the jury. The jurors were out only four hours (one of them for lunch) before bringing in a unanimous verdict in my favor. An embarrassed *Washington Post* buried the story. In its 4 July 2002 edition, the news was relegated to section B, page 2, sandwiched between an article about a man found dead in his car and a story about a camp counselor charged in a boating accident. Imagine the front-page news it would have been had I lost!

Here is how watergate.com, the definitive website on Watergate, reported it:

> After four hours of deliberation, a federal jury in Baltimore ruled in favor of G. Gordon Liddy in a $5 million defamation of character suit brought by former Democratic National Committee secretary Ida "Maxie" Wells. Wells claimed that Liddy hurt her reputation when he linked the infamous Watergate burglary to a call-girl ring. The jury was not asked to decide whether it believed the alternate Watergate theory, which portrays the burglars as looking for photos of prostitutes and not just political dirt. But in their verdict, the jurors found that Liddy did not defame Wells by repeating it.
>
> ### Dean's Role in the Wells Suit
>
> In 1997, John Garrick, a lawyer for John Dean in the Dean v. Liddy suit, urged Wells to file suit shortly before the statute of limitations expired. Another attorney for Dean in the same suit, David M. Dorsen, represented Wells in this trial. Dorsen had also served as an attorney on the Senate Watergate committee in 1973. Courthouse rumors have it that John Dean himself played an integral part in Wells' legal team in this case. In his comments concerning the verdict, Dean stated, "I'm almost speechless, because I don't understand how a jury could

find it is not defamatory to say Maxie Wells was helping run a call-girl ring." Wells was visibly upset by the ruling, tearfully stating, "There's no justice in the world. I just can't understand it." Dean himself brought suit against Liddy in 1992 but dismissed the suit in 2000.

In the trial, Liddy counsel John B. Williams sought to prove that the Watergate call-girl theory was grounded in fact. He introduced a report showing that one of the burglars was carrying a key to Wells' desk at the time of the arrest and offered circumstantial evidence linking a high-class prostitution ring at the Columbia Plaza Apartments to the DNC at the nearby Watergate office complex. In his closing arguments on July 3rd, Williams concluded that the many dueling versions of Watergate should continue to be freely and openly debated without fear of lawsuits. Liddy said he was convinced by Len Colodny, author of "Silent Coup," that Dean was behind the burglary. After visiting Colodny for four days and reviewing paperwork, Liddy said he realized he had been out of the loop. This is Liddy's third victory in the case. The judge dismissed the first trial and the initial appeal ended in mistrial when the jury deadlocked seven to two in Liddy's favor. History was preserved and changed; the "call girl ring theory" remains the only plausible theory of the Watergate break-in that has been tested by the courts.

In his dismissal of the jury, District Judge Frederic N. Smalkin thanked them for their service, saying: "You have in a sense become a part of the history of Watergate."

Liddy responded that it was a "great day for the First Amendment."

When I was a kid and this was a free country, we were free to debate our history without fear of lawsuits for defamation from those involved in that history. Thanks to Judges Motz and Smalkin, a jury of American citizens in Baltimore, and two superb trial lawyers, John Williams and Kerrie Hook, and their team, we still can.

It has taken ten years and the expenditure of great energy and treasure to crush the Watergate rat, John Dean. It is personally gratifying, of course—but far more important, I did it for the First Amendment to our Constitution, the American people, and our freedom to discover and disclose the truth of our history.

ACKNOWLEDGMENTS

I WANT TO THANK THE FOLLOWING for their assistance with this book: my son Tom Liddy for hours of research; my executive producer, Diana Kalandros, for hours of work outside her job description; Jed Donahue and Patricia Bozell for their excellent editing skills; and my friend and publisher, Al Regnery, for making the whole project possible.

INDEX